# CIVIL WAR
## MILLEDGEVILLE

# CIVIL WAR
# MILLEDGEVILLE

TALES FROM THE

Confederate Capital of Georgia

## HUGH T. HARRINGTON

THE
History
PRESS

Published by The History Press
Charleston, SC 29403
www.historypress.net

*Cover photo:* Left to right, Milledgeville residents Archibald C. McKinley, John R. Bonner, McKinley's slave Scott, William Spivey Stetson, all of Company H, 57$^{th}$ Georgia Infantry. *Courtesy Special Collections, Georgia College and State University Library.*
*Back cover photo:* Edwin F. Jemison, 2$^{nd}$ Louisiana Volunteer Infantry, *Courtesy Library of Congress.*

First published 2005
Second printing 2008


978-1-5402-0378-6

Library of Congress Cataloging-in-Publication Data

Harrington, Hugh T. (Hugh Thompson)
Civil War Milledgeville : tales from the Confederate capital of Georgia /
Hugh T. Harrington.
p. cm.
Includes index.
ISBN 1-59629-053-6 (alk. paper)
1. Milledgeville (Ga.)--History--19th century--Anecdotes. 2.
Georgia--History--Civil War, 1861-1865--Anecdotes. I. Title.
F294.M6H49 2005
975.8'04--dc22
2005011678

*To:*

*My great-grandfathers,*
*William Henry Harrington, Cadet Corporal, Company A, Georgia Military Institute, CSA*
*Hugh Smith Thompson, Captain, Company A, The Citadel Cadets, CSA*

*My great-great-grandfather,*
*Alfred Flournoy Zachry, Captain, Company F, 61ˢᵗ Alabama Infantry, CSA*

*My father,*
*William Henry Harrington, Colonel, United States Army Air Forces*

# CONTENTS

# PREFACE

THE CIVIL WAR AND MILLEDGEVILLE, Georgia, are indisputably linked. As Milledgeville was the capital of Georgia from 1804 to 1868, one cannot study the history of Milledgeville and ignore the Civil War. Equally, one cannot study the Civil War without considering the events and individuals connected with Milledgeville.

There are aspects of the Civil War, as with all wars, that are objectionable and even offensive. To ignore the distasteful would be dishonest. One must see the good and the bad, the heroism and the cowardice, the altruism and the selfishness.

It is my intention to tell the stories of people and events that are not generally covered in history books. They have been overlooked by others, sometimes because they were considered too local for a broad sweep of history or because the stories were unknown and forgotten.

Readers of the *Baldwin Bulletin* will recognize some of these chapters as having appeared, perhaps in a somewhat different form, in my "'Round and About" columns. However, many of the chapters were written especially for this volume.

While many primary and secondary sources were used, a great deal of the information presented here appeared in the newspapers during and after the war. Much of the material for the chapters on General Sherman and Brown Hospital in Milledgeville came from Dr. Robert J. Massey's articles, which appeared in the *Sunny South* and the [Atlanta] *Constitution* in 1901–1905.

The reader will not find in this book great truths or earthshaking historical revelations. What he will find is a collection of stories that are likely unknown to the average reader. It is my hope that the stories will be both entertaining as well as enlightening. Perhaps they will even encourage readers to do some historical sleuthing on their own. History can be fascinating and enjoyable. History can also demonstrate that the men and women of our past are not just dim figures on a far-off stage. They are very much like us with their own preconceived ideas, their struggles with decisions, big and small, and their living with the consequences of those decisions.

Hugh T. Harrington

# ACKNOWLEDGEMENTS

I HAVE BEEN FORTUNATE IN HAVING so many people contribute to the creation of this book. Some passed along leads to interesting stories. Others provided much needed encouragement, support and technical or research advice. A few supplied me with source materials and actively helped research some of the topics.

I want to particularly thank Nancy Davis Bray, the University Archivist of Georgia College & State University, and Tammy Wyatt, Archival Associate, for their eagerness to supply whatever I needed in the way of sources or images; also, Mary Moore Jones, Head of Interlibrary Loan, for her determined efforts to locate Dr. Robert J. Massey's eyewitness accounts of General Sherman in Milledgeville. James C. Turner, Director, Old Governor's Mansion, provided images. Eileen Babb McAdams has contributed many worthwhile suggestions as well as research. Alexa Filipowski worked with me on the Private Edwin F. Jemison chapter.

Anne Buckner Burgamy, while acting as my consultant on all aspects of the Civil War, could not have been more helpful or encouraging. Others who have helped in many ways are Louise Horne, Betty Dawson and Floride Gardner. Pam Beer, editor of the *Baldwin Bulletin*, graciously included my column, "'Round and About," in the pages of her newspaper.

Most importantly, I want to thank my wife Sue. She proofread and corrected each chapter. She also worked her magic on the images. Her continuous support, help, encouragement and patience enabled this book to become reality. Without her, there simply would have been nothing.

# SNOVEY JACKSON:
# A LOST VOICE
# FROM MILLEDGEVILLE'S PAST

S NOVEY JACKSON IS NOT A name that many in Milledgeville will recognize. Those with very long memories may recall her as an elderly black woman who lived on the northeast corner of Hancock and Jackson Streets. This would have been before 1940.

Her name appears in the Library of Congress's collection of the Slave Narratives accumulated by the Federal Writers' Project of the Works Progress Administration (WPA) in the 1930s. The goal of the project was to collect the oral personal histories of elderly people concerning the recollections of their lives and slavery.

The narratives are typed. However, as the interviewers did not have access to tape recorders, they attempted the laborious task of phonetically spelling out the narratives as spoken by the elderly subjects.

Snovey Jackson was one of 2,500 people who were interviewed nationwide. (Others from Milledgeville include Carrie Mason and Ferebe Rogers.) The interview occurred in the spring of 1937. At that time Snovey Jackson was handicapped and bent with rheumatism, living in the heart of a respectable neighborhood.

There are rewards for struggling through the odd phonetic spellings of the narratives. It is one thing to read that "General Sherman came through Milledgeville" in a tourist pamphlet or history book; it is entirely something else to read the words of a witness, Snovey Jackson, translated into proper spelling for easier reading: "We heard the Yankees were coming, and did they ruin everything! Why Milledgeville was just torn up; wasn't nothing more than a cow pasture when the Yankees got through with it. They took all the stock and cattle that folks had, and burned and destroyed everything." While this was not historically correct, it is the perception this woman had seventy years after the event.

Snovey started working for the Central Georgia Railroad about 1877 and remained on the job for fifty years. She would "get up every morning and cook breakfast for all the section hands, then I'd go to the house and cook for the family." Initially she worked for Mrs. Ann Bivins, who moved away, telling Snovey, "If I had the money, nothing but death could separate me and you." She then worked for the Nisbets.

Clearly, this woman worked hard. As she says, "I just worked myself to death." She said in her narrative that she wanted to own some land in Milledgeville. The land she wanted belonged to Mrs. Ann DuBignon. Snovey went to see Mrs. DuBignon's son, a lawyer, about the land but was told, "Snovey, you can't buy that lot. You don't have a chance in the world to pay for it."

Not satisfied with that brushoff, she walked to Scottsboro and talked to Mrs. DuBignon herself. She was told that the land was for sale but Mrs. DuBignon wanted to be paid in full and would not accept years of small payments. Snovey said that she "studied and studied, and I figured and figured, and my little wages for a whole year, even if I didn't spend a penny was mighty little." She then visited Mr. Samuel Walker, who "owned just about all the land in Baldwin County." He obtained this land by loaning money to people who put up land as security and could not pay the debt, so were forced to turn the land over to Walker. Samuel Walker loaned the money to Snovey so she could buy the property from Mrs. DuBignon.

After a year, says Snovey's narrative, "Here comes Mr. Walker, 'Well, Snovey, how you getting along?'" "I'm getting along fine Mr. Walker," replied Snovey. "What are you going to do about this land?" asked Sam Walker. Snovey "was ready for him. He thought he was going to come down and take the land, because he knew I did not have the money to pay it off. But I was waiting for him." "I'm ready, Mr. Walker, to settle up," she told him proudly. "Was he surprised! He sure was disappointed."

I checked the records on the property. On March 19, 1883, Ann DuBignon transferred the land to Snovey Jackson. Sam Walker signed a quitclaim deed to Snovey on January 1, 1884.

This was desirable property. Snovey sold off parcels as "Judge Allen persuaded me to sell him enough to build his home. Then Mr. Bone wanted to build here. So you see I have sold off several lots, and I still own part of my square. This old nigger has been the foundation of those homes you see there." When a contractor was building a fine house on what had been her part of her property, he asked Snovey to sell him her corner lot. She laughed and replied, "I might eat the goose that ate the grass that grew on your grave." The contractor died "some years ago." On June 18, 1936, Snovey transferred her property to Mrs. Willie Thomas Bone with the stipulation that Snovey could live there for life.

My friend and Milledgeville historian Floride Gardner remembers Snovey. She recalls her as being a heavy old woman whom everyone liked and called "Aunt Snovey." The WPA interviewer, Ruth A. Chitty, also called her "Aunt Snovey."

The elderly Snovey said, "I could be a grand counselor now. If I could live my days over I would show them all something. Like a rolling stone, up and down, so the world is going to move on. I have been a lot of help to folks in my day. I done made a way out of no way." The interviewer commented that the years have "bequeathed her a kindly manner and a sincere interest in the fairness and justice of things. Wisdom and judgment are tempered with a sense of humor."

Less than three years after this interview, Snovey Jackson died. She was about 92 years old. She was laid to rest in Memory Hill Cemetery beneath a high-quality marble stone. Her grave is located on the west side, Section N, Lot 7, person #4. The inscription reads, "Sonovia Jackson, January 12, 1940." It is unknown where "Sonovia" originated. In the narrative she was very clear that she considered her name "Snovey." The *Union Recorder* did not publish an obituary.

However, the January 25, 1940 edition of the *Union Recorder* carried a letter to the editor which took the place of an obituary. It was written by A.D. Nisbet, from Florida.

Mr. Nisbet wrote a long letter describing his close association with Snovey Jackson. Nisbet said he was married on May 4, 1882, and moved into the residence of the Central Railroad, and Snovey changed her employment from the Bivins family to his own on that date. Snovey lived with the Nisbet family continuously until he retired on May 2, 1923.

She had no family. "She read her bible which she cherished and loved very keenly. She was a devoted member of Flagg Chapel Church."

He said that Snovey "was a splendid good woman, no one ever heard of a single blemish on her most excellent character, her loyalty or fidelity. She was as firm as the Rock of ages...All of my children loved Snovey with a devotion almost equaling kinship, as she had lived with us such a long time. She was the bookkeeper and treasurer of each child, and kept all of their dimes and nickels with perfect accuracy."

In May of 1923 the Nisbets moved to Florida. They begged Snovey to go with them. She told them she "was no good, and too old to change homes and was unable to work." Nisbet told her "that she was a member of my family and if she would go, I would fix her up comfortably, and she would never have to work any more. She thanked us sincerely, but said she was too old to make the change."

Mr. Nisbet ends his letter, "And now, that good woman, Snovey Jackson, has gone to her maker, and is at rest. Her death was of course not a surprise, for she was an old woman. But it brought sorrow to all of my family, and had some one notified us by wire in time, we would have attended her funeral."

The story of Snovey Jackson is one of many local personalities that have almost been lost to history. Memory Hill Cemetery has over seven thousand such people, and each has a story.

# GENERAL GEORGE P. DOLES
## AND HIS MONUMENT
## IN MEMORY HILL CEMETERY

WHEN SEARCHING FOR HISTORY IN Milledgeville, it's hard to beat Memory Hill Cemetery. Even after spending hundreds of hours there I still see something new, or see something in a new way, on each visit. A stroll along the shaded lanes is rewarded by an irresistible number of gravestones that grab my attention as if to say, "I have a story to tell!" One such stone belongs to General George Doles (see photo on page 66).

Doles Monument is located on the east side, Section E, Lot 13. Brochures provided by the Friends of Baldwin County Cemeteries are located in the gazebo just to the left of the gate as you enter and contain maps that will help you find your way. Doles's grave is easy to find. Walk directly south from the main gate and turn left at the fourth cemetery road on the left. Doles will be about one hundred feet down that road on the left side.

George Doles was born in Milledgeville on May 14, 1830. He joined the Baldwin Blues as a young man and was selected as Captain in 1860. When the Baldwin Blues were absorbed into the Fourth Georgia Regiment in 1861, he was elected Colonel. He served with conspicuous gallantry in the great battles in Virginia. After the battle of Sharpsburg he was promoted to Brigadier General.

In May of 1864, at the battle of Spotsylvania, his brigade lost about a thousand men: all killed, wounded or missing. At least one Richmond newspaper criticized his brigade for falling back, despite battlefield necessities. Doles was hurt by these charges and may have been influenced by them later when in the battle at Cold Harbor, Virginia, he exposed himself, perhaps unnecessarily, to enemy fire. He was shot through the chest on June 1 and died the following day.

News and events traveled fast, perhaps faster than we would think they would 140 years ago. Doles died on June 2, 1864, a Thursday, in Virginia. His body was sent back to Milledgeville for burial. The day after his death there were rumors in Milledgeville that General Doles had been killed. On Monday, June 6, a committee of citizens met at the city council chambers to make arrangements for the ceremony to honor the fallen local hero.

At 7:00 a.m. on Tuesday, June 7, Doles's body reached Milledgeville on a special train from Gordon. At 9:00 a.m. it was "attended from the depot to the residence of the General's family, by a large number of personal friends and the Committees of Reception and Arrangements." At 10:00 a.m. it was taken to the Representative Chamber of the State House (Old Capital Building) where it was to lie in state until 5:00 p.m. The hall was draped in mourning and the coffin was placed in the center.

At the head of the coffin stood the "bullet torn battle flag of the Fourth Georgia Regiment." At the foot of the coffin were stacked the battle flags of the enemy captured in battle by the Fourth Georgia. A wreath of myrtle lay upon the coffin along with the General's sword and the flag of the Baldwin Blues.

At 5:00 p.m. a huge crowd gathered in the State House to participate in the funeral service. The service was conducted by the ministers from both the Methodist and Presbyterian churches. At the close of the service a large series of thunderstorms swept the area, causing a postponement of the funeral procession and burial until the following day. An honor guard was placed over the casket for the night.

The following morning at nine o'clock the procession was formed by Dr. Samuel G. White and Robert A. McComb, in the following order: music, chaplain, hearse, pall bearers, members of the Baldwin Blues, family, military escort, officers and soldiers of the CSA and State of Georgia, young ladies with wreaths, clergy, Committee of Reception, Committee of Arrangements, State House officers, Judges of Superior and Inferior Courts, mayor, aldermen, citizens on foot and citizens in carriages. This long procession was said to be the largest ever seen in Milledgeville. Upon leaving the Capital Square it went north on Wayne Street to Green Street, then to Liberty Street and into the cemetery. The graveside ceremony was short.

Visitors to the cemetery will notice that next to General Doles is buried his daughter Minnie. She died May 4, 1886 of consumption (tuberculosis) at the age of twenty-six. The previous year the Veterans of the Fourth Georgia held a reunion in Milledgeville. At that time, they passed a resolution naming Minnie "the daughter of the Regiment."

On the other side of General Doles is buried his wife, Sarah, "the mother of the Regiment." She died July 26, 1889, also of consumption. She was sixty years old. At the time of her death, none of the three graves was marked.

It was during the reunion of the Fourth Georgia Regiment in 1892 that a resolution was adopted to erect a monument to General Doles. It was requested that each of the ten companies that made up the Fourth Georgia contribute twenty-five dollars to the project.

In April of 1894 the contract for the Doles Monument was awarded to the marble works of Theodore Markwater of Augusta. The monument was to be unveiled at the reunion of the Fourth Georgia Regiment in July. It is described as having

> the name Doles on the second base in square cut raised letters, three quarters of an inch in relief. The dye block polished on four sides, is inscribed with square sunk chased letters, the lettering being as distinct as if each one was of polished brass, the lines as sharply defined as if of steel. The contrast between the smooth cut surface of the granite and the dark blue polish being the desideratum long sought in granite. Upon the molded cap lies in granite the counterpart of the sheathed sword which General Doles carried when killed. It is partly supported in its position by a pyramid of three grape-shot, making a very effective grouping. The hilt of the sword is cut in alto relieve, being undercut until entirely free. The scabbard is in alto relieve. The basket of the hilt is polished and traced, as are the bands around the scabbard.

Clearly, this was a magnificent piece of stonework. The cost was $375.75.

The monument was unveiled and dedicated on July 25, 1894. That morning, a train bearing the veterans arrived in Milledgeville amid a salvo of artillery fired by the cadets of the Middle Georgia Military and Agricultural College. The veterans, three hundred strong, were taken to the Court House (at that time the "new" Court House, now the "old" Court House) for a day of speeches and camaraderie before proceeding to the cemetery for the unveiling. Stores closed at 4:00 p.m. so everyone could attend. After more speechmaking, poetry and the firing of salutes, the monument was unveiled by the son of Doles's adjutant, in whose arms Doles had died thirty years before.

The Doles Monument today is weathered and discolored by well-intentioned but improper cleaning, but it still commands attention. The members of the Fourth Georgia who contributed to it would be pleased to know that the monument is still sought out by visitors to Memory Hill. The newspaper in July 1894 perhaps said it best: "Around the tomb of Doles will cluster a peculiar historic charm that falls to the lot of few men. In years to come people will gather around this sacred spot and the story of the gallant service and heroic death of Doles will be told."

# VANISHED WITHOUT A TRACE:
## THE MYSTERY OF AGNES FISH,
### CONFEDERATE SOLDIER

CEMETERIES BY THEIR VERY NATURE are mysterious to some extent. However, there are instances where what is *not* in the cemetery can be more mysterious than what is there. An apparent Confederate soldier named Agnes Fish is one of these.

In 1896, Milledgeville City Council appointed a committee consisting of J.A. Horne, L.H. Andrews and R.L. Wall to "ascertain and locate the graves of Confederate soldiers buried in the city cemetery with a view of marking the same with marble slabs."

"This work required the searching of records and a great deal of correspondence." Thirty years had passed since the end of the Civil War and many of the veterans had died and were buried in Memory Hill. The committee sought information on these veterans as well as donations from private individuals to cover the cost of the tombstones.

Because of this effort, the majority of the tombstones of Confederate soldiers in Memory Hill are of the pattern established in 1896. They can easily be recognized as they are made of marble two inches thick and twelve inches wide with curved tops. Most of the former soldiers had been buried without tombstones and so their only markers are those erected in 1896.

However, there are Confederates with a different style of grave marker. Since 1929, the U.S. government has provided gravestones, free of charge, for the graves of Confederate soldiers. These gravestones are marble and four inches thick, twelve inches wide and have a pointed top. Similar stones, except with rounded tops, are available for Union veterans of the Civil War as well as veterans of all other U.S. military service.

An interesting sidelight to the 1896 Confederate grave-marking project is that the committee also ordered tombstones for three veterans of the Union army, paid for by the donations of the citizens of Milledgeville.

The project to identify the soldiers, their units and their grave locations took place from January to April 1896. Periodically, the newspaper would print a list of the dead soldiers and their units and would ask readers to help by supplying corrections or additions to the list.

The last list printed is tantalizing, as the name Agnes Fish appears. After her name there is no unit designation as is included with almost all of the other names. A female Confederate soldier! The story immediately becomes more interesting.

A few weeks later, the stones were ordered and installed in the cemetery. If there ever was a tombstone for Agnes Fish, it was not there in the 1930s when the cemetery was first surveyed. And it is not there now.

Therein lies the mystery. Who was Agnes Fish? What service to the Confederacy did she provide that caused her name to appear on the list? Was she related to the Fish family who owned the legendary brick vault in Memory Hill? Was Fish her married name or her maiden name? When did she die? For what reason was her name not included on the final tombstone order which prevented her from getting a marker? Was she not buried here? Was she not dead in 1896? Was there something about her service that did not merit a stone? Many questions immediately come to mind, but no answers have been found to any of them.

I have spent a considerable amount of time looking for Agnes Fish and have turned up nothing. Not a trace. Not a single reference to her name. So, the question remains: who was the mysterious Agnes Fish?

# BENJAMIN WARD, BALDWIN COUNTY'S LAST CONFEDERATE VETERAN

PERHAPS IT'S SPENDING SO MUCH time playing with various history problems (my friends more likely will say it's because I'm getting old), but 1940 just doesn't seem that long ago. True, that date is before I was born, but not that many years before. So when "1940" and "Confederate" are seen together, "1940" leaps out at me as being entirely too current to be associated with "Confederate." However, in Baldwin County, 1940 has a special significance, as it was in 1940 that the last Confederate veteran died. Of the hundreds of local men who marched off to war in the 1860s, by February 1940 there was only one left: Benjamin C. Ward.

Benjamin Ward was born December 12, 1847, in Butts County, Georgia. As a child, he was taught in his home by William Seward, who became secretary of state in President Lincoln's Cabinet.

Ward enrolled in the Georgia Military Institute in Marietta, Georgia. He was a student until March 20, 1864, when the cadets entered into active service with the Confederate forces. He was in Company A, along with my great grandfather William Henry Harrington, by the way. Some time after September 1864, he left GMI and enlisted in the Confederate army. Ward became a private in Company H, First Kentucky Cavalry. He served in Tennessee, Georgia, North Carolina and South Carolina.

After the war, he went to Texas for a few years. He then went back to Butts County. He moved to Milledgeville about 1920. He was a watchman at Georgia State College for Women for eight years, retiring when he was eighty. For the twelve years before his death he was justice of the peace in Baldwin County.

He was a member of George Doles's Camp no. 730, United Confederate Veterans (UCV), serving as treasurer and also commander. He was commissioned as a Brigadier

General of the UCV as Commander of the East Georgia Division. In later years he was made an honorary member of Camp Dan Sanford, Sons of Confederate Veterans. When he was the last survivor in Baldwin County, he was the guest of honor on several occasions at the Robert E. Lee Chapter of the United Daughters of the Confederacy. He was an enthusiastic supporter of all Confederate heritage organizations.

Judge Ward died after hitting his head when he fell off his back porch on February 17, 1940. He lingered until February 29. Until his final illness, he was an active member of the Men's Bible Class of the Baptist Church. Despite being ninety-two years old, he walked to and from his office in the courthouse twice each day where he conducted his business as justice of the peace. He would also go through the business section of Milledgeville, stopping to visit with his many friends.

After his death, the Civil War seemed to become more distant. No longer was there a man who had "been there." With his death, Milledgeville lost not only a fine old gentleman but also a link with its past.

# You Mean There Are
# Yankees in Here?

I WAS WALKING WITH A FRIEND in Memory Hill Cemetery a few weeks ago. This friend is a lifelong resident of Milledgeville. As we'd pass by interesting people or tombstones I'd make a few comments about them. We passed the grave of a Union soldier and I pointed it out. His immediate reaction was, "You mean there are Yankees in here?!" He wasn't upset that the sacred soil had been somehow corrupted. He was simply shocked that, after living here for fifty years, he never knew that there were Yankees in the cemetery.

Tradition maintains that there are three Union soldiers in the cemetery, but it seems likely that there are several more. I should hurry to point out that none of these men was involved in the war locally. They came here after the war and when they died they were buried in the cemetery.

In 1896, a fund was established to pay for marble markers for the Confederate veterans who were buried in the cemetery. Along with the Confederates, three Union veterans were also marked. Their gravestones are identical to the 1896 pattern Confederate tombstones except they have USA on them rather than CSA. The three men with the 1896 markers are David Jones, George Henry Pratt and Merritt Wilson.

David Jones's marker says that he is in Company I, Thirty-third Connecticut Infantry. This presents a problem, as Connecticut did not have a Thirty-third Infantry regiment. A search of the records for burials from 1869 to 1904 does not list David Jones. He may have been buried during one of the short periods when no records of burials have survived. I have not been able to find an obituary for him. A search of the National Park Service website identifies 429 men named David Jones in the Union army. Only one was in a regiment numbered thirty-three—the Thirty-third Wisconsin Infantry. Might this be our man? I can't help but wonder, whoever he was, what he was doing here, and when he died.

The story of George Henry Pratt, of Company C, Thirteenth Connecticut Battalion, is a very sad one. In April of 1891 he brought his wife by train from Atlanta to put her into the State Hospital. The newspaper says that "Mrs. Pratt is not only very crazy but entirely helpless, her lower limbs being paralyzed." She was a daughter of Mrs. A.I. Butts of Milledgeville. After leaving his wife at the State Hospital, Captain Pratt went to the Butts home where he was to spend the night. He was naturally despondent and lamented the fate of his wife. He took a dose of something before going to bed. The next morning he was found to be in a comatose condition and died before noon. The coroner's investigation disclosed that he had taken morphine, which had caused his death. However, it was not thought that the morphine was taken with the intention of committing suicide. Pratt was from Bridgeport, Connecticut. After the war he had taken a job with the U.S. government in Macon and married Ada Hutchings, a daughter of Rebecca Hutchings, who later became Mrs. A.I. Butts. Ada Pratt died in 1910.

The third Union soldier in Memory Hill is Merritt Wilson of Company D, Third Michigan Infantry. He died June 30, 1880. He was visiting his brother Carlos G. Wilson, who was the postmaster at Milledgeville, when he died suddenly of heart disease at the age of thirty-five.

Lying in an unmarked grave is Merritt Wilson's brother, Union soldier Carlos G. Wilson. He died in 1906. He had been in the Second Michigan Cavalry during the war. As a side note, Merritt and Carlos Wilson had a brother, Horace, who was also a Union veteran. Horace, part owner of the Wilson & Meadows grocery store, engaged in a gunfight with Frederick McComb and Gordon McComb at the store in 1874. Frederick McComb was killed. Horace Wilson was sentenced to four years in the penitentiary. He returned to Michigan.

There is a fifth man in Memory Hill who is said to have been a Union soldier. The Allen-Andrews Directory, which was compiled in the 1930s, indicates that Columbus Wilcox belonged to the Sixth Connecticut Regulars. It does not say so on his gravestone and I have been unable to verify his service. He died in 1883 but does not have an 1896 pattern tombstone as was placed on the graves of all known veterans at that time. His obituary states he was born in New York in 1802 and moved to New Orleans in 1830. During the war, he lost his property when the Federal troops occupied New Orleans. He fled to Arkansas and later wanted to return to New Orleans. So, alone, he took a skiff three hundred miles down the Arkansas and Mississippi rivers. In going past besieged Vicksburg, he dodged shot and shell in his little boat. He said it was his duty to return. These do not sound like the actions of a Union soldier, and I suspect he was never in the Union army. Perhaps his service in the Sixth Connecticut was during the Mexican War, which, given his age, seems far more likely.

No doubt other former Union soldiers were also buried locally. I would find it interesting to know their stories and how they came to be here.

# THE BRAVE AND TRIUMPHANT MARCH OF SERGEANT BATES

BY EARLY 1868, THE CIVIL War had been over for almost three years. However, the hard feelings, poverty and near famine conditions were clearly evident in the South. Some thought that the South, though beaten militarily, could never again be trusted or considered part of the Union. Others believed that the South did consider itself part of the Union and was loyal to the flag.

This debate led to a wager among several former Union soldiers in Wisconsin. Former sergeant of the First Wisconsin Heavy Artillery, Gilbert H. Bates, was confident that the South had returned to the Union in spirit as well as in fact. He was willing to put his life on the line to prove it.

The wager was that Sergeant Bates was to walk alone, from Vicksburg, Mississippi to Washington, D.C., carrying the American flag, unfurled for all to see. He was to carry no weapons. He was neither permitted to carry any money nor to accept money from anyone on the march. He was forced to depend upon Southern hospitality to be his only source of food and shelter.

Many thought he was committing suicide. Mark Twain called him an "ass" and predicted that Bates would get "more black eyes, down there among those unreconstructed rebels." It seemed foolhardy to carry the flag of the victor fourteen hundred miles through the war-torn area, devastated by General Sherman, where daily hardship was routine. It did not seem so to Bates, who stated that he believed "no one will touch me."

In January, dressed in farmers' clothes, he took the train to war-scarred Vicksburg to begin his trek. He carried his Wisconsin regimental flag. On the train, he was asked by another passenger what he was doing. He gave his explanation. The passenger put him up in a hotel in Vicksburg. Shortly afterwards the mayor and a group of prominent men appeared at his door. The mayor gave an official dinner for him. Ladies sewed him a new silk American flag.

Bates left Vicksburg in triumph, with a parade, a brass band and cheering crowds of well-wishers sending him off. Soon, however, he was in the countryside walking alone with his flag. It was cold and snowing. Late in the afternoon, he came upon a man who demanded to know what he was doing with the flag. Bates told him. Without a word the man took off his overcoat and placed it over Bates's shoulders, then stepped back and saluted. He then vanished without a word.

Bates managed to average about sixteen miles per day. Everywhere he went he was welcomed into private homes or put up in hotels. He was asked to give speeches and his hand was continually shaken by young and old alike. While walking along one desolate stretch of road next to train tracks, he was astounded to see a passenger train stop next to him so the passengers and crew could get off to shake his hand. The conductor forced money into his pocket, saying it was for postage stamps so he could write home to tell his Northern friends that Southerners were "all fired Americans."

In Meridian, Mississippi, he was paraded through town in the back of a carriage while people cheered. Days later, out on a country road, he came upon twenty ladies who were waiting for him. They had prepared a dinner in his honor.

The *New York Times* said in an editorial, "joyful multitudes everywhere hail his advance as though it were the advance of an Emperor." He was asked to visit a dying former Confederate officer, which he did. Later, he was asked if he would visit the grave of a Confederate soldier killed in the war. He prayed with the soldier's family at the grave. A former Confederate soldier handed him a tattered American flag, saying that it had been taken in battle but that "you have recaptured it without firing a shot."

Sergeant Bates arrived at Milledgeville at 4:00 p.m. on March 5. He was met at the edge of town by over thirty citizens who escorted him to the Milledgeville Hotel. He stayed here all day Friday before leaving Saturday morning for Sparta, which he expected to reach before night. The *Southern Recorder* newspaper described Bates as an "open, frank and agreeable man."

The *Southern Recorder* was sure that "Sergeant Bates can go through the entire South without the least fear from the Southern people, not only that, he will meet with kind treatment." However, the paper cautioned that if Bates were killed during his march it would be done by the Radicals who were running the governments of the Southern states. The Radicals feared that if Bates could go through the South in peace he would show that the Radicals were wrong in taking the position that the South was unruly and needed to be punished and ruled with an iron hand.

Bates marched on. When he reached South Carolina, there was a group of twenty-five Confederate veterans to greet him at the border. The veterans escorted him to

Columbia, where Bates wrote in his diary that he "shook hands with every man in Columbia today, I think, and with several of them more than once."

When Bates reached Washington, D.C., he was greeted with crowds, cheers and a brass band which escorted him to the White House where President Andrew Johnson met him on the front steps. Bates's march from Vicksburg, through Milledgeville, to Washington, as a demonstration of the good will and unity of the United States, was successfully completed.

# The Misspelled Tombstone of Dr. Andrew J. Foard, CSA, Nearly Causes Him to Be Forgotten

In the center of Memory Hill Cemetery, next to the large granite marker indicating to visitors where the original Methodist Church once stood, is the grave of one of Milledgeville's more noteworthy citizens, Dr. Andrew J. Foard. Unfortunately, in 1896, when the graves of Confederate soldiers were being marked, the name on his tombstone was misspelled. It reads "Ford" instead of "Foard." That missing letter "a" makes all the difference in being recognized and being forgotten.

Curiously, Dr. Foard hasn't been completely forgotten by at least one visitor to the cemetery. At some point since 1998, when the cemetery was indexed, a small granite marker with "Andrew J. Foard" carved on it has been cemented to his slab. I would guess that it was placed by a descendant who went to a great deal of trouble to locate him.

The misspelled Confederate marker says that he was a "surgeon in General Johnston's Army." He was much more than simply a surgeon. Dr. Foard became the Medical Director of the Army of Tennessee. He was mentioned by General Braxton Bragg, who wrote, "The high professional attainments of this admirable officer, united to his gentleness of manner, kindness of heart, and untiring zeal, peculiarly adapt him for the very important post he fills with so much credit to himself and satisfaction to this Army." In February 1865, he was promoted from Medical Director of the Army of Tennessee to Medical Inspector of the armies and hospitals in the States of Georgia, Florida, Alabama and Mississippi.

Before the war, he was an assistant surgeon in the U.S. Army. He resigned April 1, 1861, and offered his services to the Confederacy. After the war, he was a professor at the Washington Medical College in Baltimore. In 1867 he was able to help some people with an unspecified problem at the request of Robert E. Lee, then president of Washington College.

While in Baltimore he became seriously ill. He went to Charleston, South Carolina, and died there on Wednesday, March 18, 1868. His body was returned to Milledgeville for burial, as this was his boyhood home. It reached Milledgeville on Friday and was taken to the home of his friend Dr. Samuel G. White, where it lay in state and was visited by his many friends before being buried on Sunday afternoon.

The Reverend William Flinn of the Presbyterian Church delivered an impressive funeral sermon before a large crowd. The funeral procession then headed to the cemetery. The clergy led the way, followed by the hearse and members of the medical profession acting as pall bearers. Next in line came a large number of young ladies with wreaths of flowers and evergreens. Bringing up the rear were citizens on foot and in carriages.

As the funeral procession reached the entrance to Memory Hill, the choirs of several churches sang a requiem. At the graveside, the Burial Service of the Church of England was read by the Reverend Malloy of the Methodist Episcopal Church. At the conclusion of the service, the young ladies, while singing a hymn, passed by and dropped their wreaths into the grave.

The *Southern Recorder* commented that "the deep and heartfelt interest manifested by those present, gave assurance of the esteem in which Dr. Foard was held by our community and evinced their desire to honor one, who born in their midst, had achieved such distinction in his profession, and rendered such important service to his country."

The *Federal Union* said that "his memory will be cherished by all who knew him." It would be proper for us to remember him as well.

# James W. Herty,
# United States Navy and
# Confederate States Navy

I N MILLEDGEVILLE IT IS UNIVERSALLY accepted that "Dr. Herty" is Dr. Charles Holmes Herty, the famous chemist. However, there was another Dr. Herty in Milledgeville who also had a very interesting life. I'm referring to Charles Holmes Herty's uncle, James William Herty.

James Herty's tombstone in Memory Hill simply says that he was a surgeon in the Confederate Navy. There is much more to his story, however.

James Herty was born August 14, 1838, in Milledgeville. After attending local schools, he went to the University of New York to study medicine. After graduation in about 1859, he joined the United States Navy as an assistant surgeon. Then came the Civil War.

Georgia seceded from the Union in January of 1861 while Dr. Herty was an officer in the U.S. Navy. He was serving aboard the United States ship *San Jacinto*, which was patrolling off the Africa coast. The next month, Georgia joined in the creation of the Confederate States of America. On April 12, 1861, the war began with the firing on Fort Sumter in Charleston harbor. In July, the battle of First Manassas set the tone for future battles in the war: they would be bloody, and the war would not be ending soon.

The *San Jacinto* was ordered to return to the United States. Upon reaching the Caribbean, Captain Wilkes, who commanded the *San Jacinto*, learned that two Confederate diplomats, John Slidell and James M. Mason, had taken passage to England on the British ship *HMS Trent*. On his own initiative, Captain Wilkes forced the *Trent* to heave to by firing two shots across her bow. Wilkes then demanded that the Captain of the *Trent* turn over the two Confederate diplomats. The Captain refused, so Wilkes ordered that the diplomats be forcibly removed from the *Trent* and taken aboard the *San Jacinto*. The stopping of a ship of a neutral country and removing passengers was against international law.

The *San Jacinto* arrived in Boston Harbor on November 24 and turned over its prisoners to local prison authorities. The *Trent* Affair, as this event became known, created an international incident. The British were outraged that their vessel had been stopped on the high seas. The Americans, initially jubilant, backpedaled and reached a diplomatic solution by apologizing and releasing the prisoners on January 1, 1862. The prisoners were put on another ship to continue their journey to England. The United States could not afford to go to war with England and did not want to antagonize the British, which might cause them to formally recognize the Confederacy.

On November 30, 1861, a week after its arrival in Boston, the *San Jacinto* was decommissioned and overhauled. It is not known if Dr. Herty was assigned to another ship immediately or not. However, on December 12, 1861, he resigned his commission in the United States Navy and stated his desire to join the Confederacy. In late December, Dr. Herty was exchanged for a United States doctor who had been held as a prisoner of war by the Confederacy. Dr. Herty then offered his services to the Confederate States of America.

Dr. Herty was assigned to the Confederate ironclad *Richmond*. The *Richmond* was launched May 6, 1862, at the Norfolk Navy Yard and immediately towed up the James River to Richmond to be completed. She was finished in July 1862 in Richmond. The *Richmond* saw no action while Herty was assigned to her.

After the *Richmond*, Dr. Herty was transferred to the CSS *Rappahannock*. The *Rappahannock* was built in England on the Thames River in 1857 for the British government and was originally named *Victor*. The ship had many mechanical defects and the British government decided to sell her. An agent of the Confederate government purchased the ship, but the British suspected she was destined to be a Confederate commerce raider rather than to be used for the China trade as the Confederate representative had suggested, so the British ordered her detention. The British did not want to be in the position of openly supplying the Confederacy with ships. On November 24, 1863, the *Rappahannock* escaped from England with workmen still on board and only a skeleton crew. Her Confederate Naval officers came aboard in the English Channel. Unfortunately, the ship burned out her engine bearings while in the English Channel and had to be towed to Calais, France. The French government detained the *Rappahannock* on various pretexts and prevented her from ever getting to sea.

During the many months that the *Rappahannock* was detained, Dr. Herty took every opportunity to tour Europe.

In 1863 and 1864, the twin screw ironclad *Stonewall* was built in France for the Confederate government. However, when she was completed, the French would not allow her delivery to the Confederacy. Instead, the ship was sold to Denmark. The ship arrived in Copenhagen after the Schleswig-Holstein War was over so the Danes refused to accept her. The Confederacy then bought the ship from the builder. In December 1864, the *Stonewall* was turned over to the Confederacy and was sailed to France to take on supplies. Dr. Herty joined the *Stonewall* on or about January 11, 1865, on the high seas along with many officers and men from the *Rappahannock*. To further maintain the secret of the ship's ownership, the *Stonewall* was called the *Staerkodder*. Later, the *Stonewall* was christened at sea in the Bay of Biscay and ran up the Confederate flag.

Soon the little ironclad was embroiled in a heavy storm. The ship would go down into the trough between waves and ever so slowly rise with the next wave, water pouring from her decks. This was very disconcerting for officers and seamen alike. Soon it was discovered that there were major leaks in the vessel. The crew had no alternative but to steam for the nearest port. After several days of battling the storm, the *Stonewall* put into the harbor of Ferrol, Spain. Here she underwent repairs and took on coal for the run to America.

While she was in Ferrol, the United States warship *Niagara* came into the harbor. Clearly, the mission of the *Niagara* was to keep watch on the *Stonewall*. Soon it was learned that another United States warship, the *Sacramento*, was in another port only a few miles away and within eyesight of Ferrol. A few days later, the *Niagara* left Ferrol and joined the *Sacramento* with the obvious intention of waiting for the *Stonewall* to leave the harbor and, once international waters were reached, to engage her in battle. Each officer of the *Stonewall* sent ashore his pocket watch to be forwarded to relatives as a last memento of his life, as it was clear that the *Stonewall* was no match for the two U.S. ships.

After being resupplied, repaired and ready for sea, there was but one thing left to do. The *Stonewall* would steam out of the harbor where she would engage in battle with the two ships. Thousands of people went up on the shoreline mountains to witness the battle that would take place just outside Spanish territorial waters, about three miles distant.

All day the *Stonewall* went back and forth, within easy visual range of the U.S. ships, but neither came out to give battle. The *Stonewall* left the area and went to Lisbon, Portugal. Here she was to pick up more coal. She had not taken on much coal in Ferrol, because to do so would have kept the bow low in the water which would have hampered her forward gun. Also, if she was to lose the battle, as was likely, she would not have needed coal.

To the surprise of everyone, the two United States vessels came into Lisbon and dropped anchor. International law forced belligerents to give opposing forces a twenty-four-hour head start if both were in the same neutral port. Thus, the *Stonewall* would have a day to get a head start on her voyage to America.

The *Stonewall* sailed to Havana where the news of the end of the war was received. The Captain gave the ship to the Spanish authorities in exchange for enough money to pay the wages of the officers and crew. They were all then discharged.

Dr. Herty returned to Milledgeville, where he was first a druggist and then a physician. He was also mayor of Milledgeville for two terms as well as a third-degree Mason and junior warden of St. Stephen's Church. He died on December 20, 1877, after a short illness.

Dr. James W. Herty, as far as I know, is the only man in Memory Hill who honorably served both the United States military and the Confederate States military during the Civil War.

# THE COURAGEOUS CAPTAINS OF
# THE BALDWIN BLUES, 1861–1865

THE BEST KNOWN OF MILLEDGEVILLE'S military companies to go off to war in 1861 was the Baldwin Blues. The company had been in existence for years, drilling and participating in parades. Beginning in the fall of 1860, it was called upon by the mayor for security during the Secession Convention of January, 1861. However, these officers and men of the Baldwin Blues were not professional soldiers. They were civilians with families, occupations and a multitude of duties and responsibilities entirely separate from any sort of military function. The time they devoted to the Baldwin Blues before the war was minimal. However, when war came, these citizen soldiers left for the front.

The first captain of the Baldwin Blues was thirty-year-old George Doles. He was captain in peacetime and the company reelected him captain on April 26, 1861, when the regiment became Company H, Fourth Georgia Regiment. Two weeks later, he was promoted to colonel of the Fourth Georgia Regiment. Doles was wounded July 1, 1862, at Malvern Hill. On June 2, 1864, he was killed at the battle of Cold Harbor. Much has been written elsewhere about him, so I won't go into any more detail about him now.

The vacancy in the company was filled by the election to captain of Jacob M. Caraker on May 9, 1861. Caraker was twenty-seven years old. He had been captain of the guard at the penitentiary in Milledgeville before the war. In April, he had been elected first lieutenant; now he commanded the company.

We are fortunate in having a firsthand account of Captain Caraker in action. One of the privates in the company, W.H. Roberts, wrote that on June 25, 1862, the Fourth Georgia had "formed an extended picket line in the Chicahominy Swamp" and was "attacked by McClellen's army." The "bullets flew so thick" as "drops of rain or hail." The regiment had no choice but to fall back. Four men, including Roberts, were not able to fall back with the others and were cut off and captured. In a futile effort to save his men, Caraker "rallied less than a dozen of the men who were in the sound of [Caraker's] voice and held the left wing of the enemy's force in check until [Caraker's] men used every round of ammunition that they had." Thirty-nine years later, Roberts wrote Caraker to remind him of that day.

Jacob Caraker was severely wounded at the battle of Sharpsburg on September 17, 1862, and was forced to resign on February 3, 1863, due to his injuries. After the war, he was in the furniture business in Milledgeville until he died November 2, 1907.

Twenty-four-year-old J. Wallace Butts replaced Caraker as captain. He had joined the Baldwin Blues as a private. He was promoted to second lieutenant July 30, 1862. Some time later he became a first lieutenant. On February 6, 1863, he took over from Caraker as captain. At the battle of Chancellorsville, May 2, 1863, he was badly wounded in his right hand. The hand was amputated except for the thumb and one finger. Butts must have been a very tough man, as he was not absent from his company for very long due to the wound. He continued in command until July 13, 1864, when he was seriously wounded in the leg and captured near Washington, D.C. His leg was amputated and he was imprisoned as a prisoner of war. How he managed to survive the wound and amputation as well as a year in a prison camp and then get back to Milledgeville can only be imagined as a story of remarkable courage.

Butts died on August 5, 1890. He left a wife and three sons, the oldest aged about fourteen. Butts's obituary said, "for some years past he has been engaged in the active duties of a farmer's life, and considering his crippled condition has made a successful farmer." He has been described as a "splendid soldier, brave to recklessness, devoted to the cause, a hero in deed and in truth."

The last captain of the Baldwin Blues was Bernard R. Herty, the father of Charles Holmes Herty. In April 1861, he was elected fourth sergeant. He was promoted to second lieutenant in December of 1862. He was wounded at Spotsylvania May 12, 1864. He may never officially have been promoted to captain. On March 11, 1865, at the very end of the war, he signed a letter as "B. R. Herty, 2nd Lt. Commanding Co. H 4th Ga." This wounded combat veteran with four years of service had just turned twenty-one years of age.

Captain Herty was treasurer of the Lunatic Asylum when he died October 7, 1878, at the age of thirty-four. He was given a big funeral. The funeral procession from Herty's home consisted of the Masons in full regalia, the trustees and officers of the Lunatic Asylum, the drum corps of the Baldwin Blues with muffled instruments and the Baldwin Blues wearing crepe on the left arm as well as on their rifles and colors. Then came representatives from the Putnam Rifles, Macon Volunteers, Floyd Rifles and Macon Cadets. Following the military was the hearse and vehicles carrying relatives and friends and family. Playing the Dead March, the procession went to St.

Stephen's church. A large crowd had assembled, many of whom were unable to get into the building. After the service, the procession, with hundreds of people on foot following behind, went to Memory Hill. At the grave the burial service was read, the Masonic rites were performed and three volleys were fired. It was the largest funeral since the first captain of the Baldwin Blues, George Doles, had been buried there in 1864.

Four ordinary citizens went to war. None were experienced soldiers. But they all were leaders. They led their men from the front and each paid the price. All were wounded; one was killed. Only Caraker lived to a reasonable age, dying at seventy-three. Butts's death at fifty-one seems premature and may have been related to his two wounds. Herty dying at age thirty-four is likely due, in some respect, to his service in the military. They were four courageous men from Milledgeville who answered the call with courage and set a high standard to which future generations can aspire.

# LOOKING FOR GEORGIA'S 1861 SECESSION FLAG

J ANUARY 1861 WAS ARGUABLY THE most exciting, noisy, chaotic and important time in the history of Milledgeville. It was then that the Secession Convention met and ultimately took Georgia out of the Union. During the Convention, Milledgeville was alive with several thousand additional people from all over the state as well as the nation. Emotions ran high. Impromptu speechmaking on street corners competed with the firing of cannons and pistols as various individuals and groups debated, celebrated, argued and drank.

As Georgia was a part of the United States, the traditional United States flag (the Stars and Stripes) was the recognized flag. However, when the Ordnance of Secession was passed, Georgia became a sovereign, independent state. The United States flag was taken down. In place of it, another flag had to be raised. Further, the street demonstrators, who had been protesting more or less continuously for days and nights, needed flags to wave.

The new flag that replaced the Stars and Stripes, with several minor variations, has become known as the Secession flag. It was white with one large, five-pointed, red star in the center of the white flag. It was similar to the Bonnie Blue flag except that instead of a blue field with a white star, the field was white and the star was red.

These flags were made locally by enthusiastic and patriotic women. The flags were paraded up and down the streets, waved from windows, and flown from the State House and governor's mansion. However, the new flags did not last long. Within a few weeks, Georgia would join with other states and become part of the Confederate States of America. Soon they would be flying the flag of the Confederate States.

With the establishment of the Confederacy and the coming of the Confederate flag, the "old" Secession flag was obsolete. As the Secession flags were replaced by

Confederate flags, their usefulness came to an end. What became of them? As they were made in Milledgeville, by local residents, it seems to me unlikely they would have ever left town. After 143 years, is it possible that there is one surviving? Perhaps its origins have become lost to the owners and its history forgotten. An original Secession flag would make a wonderful addition to a local museum.

# Two Milledgeville Men Join the U.S. Navy during the Civil War

We often talk about some of the local men and women who served the Confederacy. There were others who thought their best interests lay with the United States and enlisted in the armed forces of the Union. At least two such men were from Milledgeville.

An eighteen-year-old black man, Fred Smith, enlisted in the U.S. Navy in Florida on January 16, 1862. He apparently had no experience with the sea or ships as he was rated "3rd Class Boy," which was a rating commonly used for underage landsmen. I don't know what his ship assignment was before December 1862, when he appears on the muster roll of the USS *Huntsville*.

The *Huntsville*, a wooden steamship, served in the Gulf of Mexico as part of the Union blockade. From 1862 to 1865 she captured at least a dozen blockade runners and assisted in the capture of others. I have not been able to determine what Fred Smith's duties on the ship were. In the spring of 1864, the *Huntsville* crew was hit hard by yellow fever. It was so bad that the ship was sent north. The muster rolls of the ship are incomplete, and the last entry for Fred Smith was in January of 1864. It is quite possible that he died from yellow fever. However, he may have survived and been transferred to other duties.

The second man from Milledgeville was nineteen-year-old Charles Batton. He enlisted in New York City on October 1, 1863, for three years. He was rated as a "1st Class Boy" and was assigned to the ship *Supply*, where he stayed for a year. If he craved a change to more exciting duty, he got his wish when he was transferred to the USS *Monadnock* in October 1864.

The *Monadnock* was a brand new ironclad of the "Monitor" type with two gun turrets. Each revolving turret contained two fifteen-inch guns that made the vessel a very formidable weapon. The *Monadnock* saw heavy combat in the battles leading up to the Union's destruction of Fort Fisher, which protected Wilmington, North Carolina.

In late 1864, Wilmington, North Carolina was the only Confederate port open where blockade runners could still take out valuable cotton and return with much-needed war materials. This was no trickle of goods, but rather a stream. In the last three months of 1864, 546,000 pairs of shoes, 8,632,000 pounds of meat, 1,506,000 pounds of lead, 316,000 blankets, 69,000 rifles and 43 cannons came through the port of Wilmington. Fort Fisher protected the mouth of Cape Fear River and allowed the blockade runners access to Wilmington.

In December of 1864 and January of 1865, Union forces were massed to destroy Fort Fisher and capture Wilmington. The *Monadnock* and four other ironclads were placed only a thousand yards offshore and began a relentless pounding of the fort. They were joined by fifty-seven other naval vessels, making this the most powerful battleship force ever assembled. A heavy bombardment and an infantry assault finally brought about the destruction of Fort Fisher.

The *Monadnock* was in the thick of the action, giving fire and receiving heavy fire in return. One of the men on the ship, a quartermaster named William Dunn, received the Medal of Honor for his actions during the battle.

After the battle at Fort Fisher, the *Monadnock*, and Charles Batton, went to Charleston to contribute to the bombardment of the defenses of that city. At the war's end, the *Monadnock* was sent to Havana, Cuba, to watch over the Confederate ironclad *Stonewall* until that ship was turned over to the U.S. government by the Cuban authorities. Charles Batton would have had no way of knowing that another man from Milledgeville, Dr. James W. Herty, had served aboard the *Stonewall*.

In the fall of 1865, Charles Batton and the *Monadnock* embarked on a remarkable journey that must have been as memorable as the assault on Fort Fisher. The *Monadnock* left Philadelphia in October, heading for California. As there was no Panama Canal, she had to take the long run south and pass through the stormy Strait of Magellan at the tip of South America before turning north again and working her way to San Francisco. She arrived in June of 1866. At that time, it was the longest voyage any ironclad had attempted.

I have no idea what became of Charles Batton. He may have stayed in California, remained in the Navy or even returned to Milledgeville. Tracing the lives of these two black men from Milledgeville would make a very interesting adventure into history. I hope someone, or perhaps a history class, takes up the challenge to learn the full story.

# Women Escape from
# Milledgeville Penitentiary

In the late winter of 1864, there occurred at the State Penitentiary in Milledgeville one of the most interesting escapes ever to have taken place at that location. Four desperate female prisoners escaped; if they had been entirely successful, they may have aided the Northern cause in the Civil War.

The four women, led by nineteen-year-old Nellie Bryan, dug a hole through the wall of their cell, giving them access to the courtyard of the prison. From there, they simply walked out of the prison. Nellie and one of the other women made men's clothes from their blankets and sheets. Dressed as men, they passed themselves off as young boys accompanying their "mother," an older female prisoner. The other prisoner made up the foursome as a female traveling companion.

The escapees took the train to Madison and from there another train to Augusta. Their goal was the Augusta Arsenal and powder works. Nellie Bryan had been convicted of attempting to set fire to houses in Macon. She was suspected of being a Federal spy. Probably because she was young, and a woman, she avoided a firing squad.

When they reached Augusta, the "mother" enlisted her two "boys" in the military company guarding the arsenal. In a real display of nerve, the "mother" wrote the captain commanding the company, asking that he take good care of her "boys" and to watch over their morals as they were young and had not seen much of the world.

The four women must have been taken completely by surprise when, at 9:00 p.m. two days after their escape, the door of the house where they were staying burst open and they found themselves in custody again. Captain Jacob M. Caraker, a prison guard who had recently commanded the Baldwin Blues until a wound had forced his resignation, had been trailing them.

Caraker sent a telegram to his anxious boss in Milledgeville: "I have caught all of the women. I will be at home tomorrow." His simple statement belied the fact that the arsenal and powder works could easily have been sabotaged by the "boys."

Upon reaching her former home in the penitentiary, Nellie Bryan faced a very difficult future. The Head Keeper was having an iron cage built to hold her. Four years were added to her sentence for escaping, plus another four years for helping others to escape. Just how long she lived in the cage and how big the cage was, I don't know.

In nine months, Sherman would be in Milledgeville and the penitentiary would be set afire and emptied of its prisoners. I cannot help but wonder what happened to Nellie Bryan and her companions. Did they go on to attempt other acts of sabotage, or had they had enough of the war? As she was nineteen in 1864, it is possible Nellie Bryan lived well into the twentieth century. What stories she would have to tell her grandchildren.

# EYEWITNESS TO SHERMAN
# IN MILLEDGEVILLE

FRIDAY, NOVEMBER 18, 1864, DAWNED cold and raw in Milledgeville. The state legislature was in session. Governor Joseph Brown (see photo on page 66) had sent a message to both houses the day before, which said in part "that a military bill of the character indicated be also passed, and that the governor and legislature then adjourn to the front to aid in the struggle till the enemy is expelled, and to meet again, if we should live, at such time and place as the governor may designate."

We are fortunate to have a witness in Dr. Robert J. Massey who was in charge of Brown Hospital in Milledgeville at this time. In 1901, he wrote about his experiences in Milledgeville. He was a keen observer with a remarkable memory and witnessed events that few others would have seen or written about.

The reaction to Governor Brown's message to the legislature was an "outburst of patriotism," inciting men to action and urging them "to repel the foul invader from the sacred soil of the red old hills of Georgia," to "fall fighting with our faces to the foe" and to "die in the last ditch," while "routing the dastardly and cowardly Hessians." One resolution that was passed on that day was introduced by F.M. Gue of Chatham County; it instructed Governor Brown to put General Joseph E. Johnston in command of the troops, "believing that his name will give confidence both to the troops and people, and rally to his standard all loyal men capable of bearing arms." Dr. Massey cynically wondered how many "loyal men" and "men capable of bearing arms" in the legislature "thus became inspired." He notes, however, that Mr. Gue did enter the armed forces and "did noble service on more battlefields than one."

For the past several weeks, rumors had flown through an anxious Milledgeville. Where Sherman was going after he left Atlanta was the question on everyone's mind.

The refugees pouring into town over the previous few days each had a tale, an opinion and a rumor to pass along. In the late morning of Friday, November 18, solid news reached Governor Brown by telegram. No longer need people worry about unfounded rumors; here was the answer to the question. Sherman's huge Union army was headed for Milledgeville and wasn't far away.

The legislators had adjourned for a midday meal, leaving their papers on their desks. After the news of the approach of Sherman became known, not a legislator returned to the State House. Massey tells us that "horses, mules, carts, buggies, carriages of all descriptions, were in great demand; price was no object; some gave as high as $1000 for conveyances 16 miles out of town." If transportation was not available they "took the 'independent people's line' and footed it... Long before night...the legislators had all, with but two or three exceptions, left the town." Massey remembered one legislator who remained: Dr. Stewart, of Rockdale County. Stewart was apparently not "in the least troubled by either the commanding general or any of his subordinates."

Dr. Massey immediately telegraphed to his superior asking for instructions. His hospital had six wards and two hundred sick, wounded and convalescents. He was told to remain with his hospital and surrender. He was to ask for protection for his patients, assistants, nurses and help. He was also ordered to send to the rear every patient able to travel, along with any medical stores and personnel he could do without.

Massey went to each ward and personally explained to the patients and staff that Sherman was approaching. Anyone able to get away was given the option of leaving town. He could not offer transportation, so his patients had to walk to safety. All but forty-eight patients left the hospital. To his surprise, "some fifteen or twenty who had not been off their bunks, except when helped off, for the last three or four weeks" got dressed and left. He wryly commented, "I have never heard from them, so far as I know they are walking still."

Governor Brown pardoned the convicts in the penitentiary. He had them help the quartermaster remove stores belonging to the state. He also formed them into a military company and selected a "celebrated burglar," Ezekiel Roberts, to be their captain. The governor then made them "a neat, beautiful, patriotic speech, referring very tenderly to the circumstances incident to their pardoning, restoration to citizenship and their duties as southern patriots."

Governor Brown, with his family, left Milledgeville about four o'clock in the afternoon on Saturday, November 19, for his home in Dooly County. Massey says that after the war, "unscrupulous correspondents" spread stories about how Governor Brown had taken away large quantities of his personal property and left state property behind to be destroyed. It was even said that Brown had loaded a cart with cabbages from his garden: "A great many unkind things were said about Joe Brown and his cabbages." Dr. Massey says he was present and the governor did not take his own property in preference to that of the state. He also states, "The fact of the case is, Governor Brown's good old mother and her old cook, Aunt Cella, wishing to provide something for them to eat while they were out camping, gathered only two basketsful of ordinary, old fashioned bluestem Georgia collards."

On Sunday, Dr. Massey learned that Union cavalry was about to enter Milledgeville. With his surgeon's commission in hand, he went to meet the invaders. In front of the governor's mansion, he encountered Captain Duncan of the Union army who politely asked what he was doing there. He explained he was under orders to surrender his hospital. Duncan then asked to see the hospital.

Dr. Massey asked Captain Duncan and "two or three of [his] friends" into Massey's office where he gave them glasses and they drank two bottles of brandy and sugar as they sat warming before his blazing fire. When they were finished, Duncan decided he didn't really need to see the hospitals and offered to provide any assistance Massey needed. He also advised his superior that Massey and his hospital were "all right" and protection should be provided for his hospital. An hour later, the cavalry left town.

The next morning, several hundred foragers, often called "bummers," came into Milledgeville. They "took everything they could find in sight that could be carried away and searched for many things that were out of sight." Brown hospital was sacked. Not a bit of food or medical supplies was left.

As soon as the regular Federal army appeared the following day, Massey went to the headquarters of General Howard. Howard referred him to Sherman. When Massey got to Sherman he found the mayor, B.B. deGraffenreid, there asking for protection for the city. Sherman was "in no very amiable mood." He spoke to the mayor using "many expletives."

There were several "old gentlemen" present who were past arm-bearing age. To these men Sherman "was kind and considerate." There were a couple of "young gentlemen" present. These men were exempt from military service due to their clerical duties. These men Sherman addressed "with a withering scowl." "Young men, you are worse than traitors to profess the principles you do and shield yourselves behind such an exemption; it is worse than treason. You should hang your head in shame and are unworthy of the consideration of any honorable gentleman or lady." Dr. Massey advises that this was a sore point for the "young gentlemen" if it was ever referred to in later years.

Sherman, "in a very pleasant manner," ordered a requisition for whatever medicines, food and supplies that Dr. Massey requested. He also provided a guard for the hospital with the unusual order that the guards should obey Dr. Massey "in preference to any of his [Sherman's] officers."

Dr. Massey, in 1901, wrote that he has "ever felt grateful" for "the many acts of kindness and courtesy that I received at the hands of General Sherman's provost marshal, Colonel William H. Hawley, Indiana Infantry."

Just before Sherman left Milledgeville he sent for Dr. Massey. He told Massey that he had twenty-eight sick men and wanted to leave them in Massey's care. Massey asked what he should do with the men when they recovered. Sherman replied, "If they die, give them a decent burial. If they live, send them to Andersonville, of course. They are prisoners of war; what else can you do? If I had your men I would send them to prison."

Sherman, and his army, then left Milledgeville.

Dr. Massey doesn't say what became of the twenty-eight Union soldiers.

# THE "FUNERAL" OF GOVERNOR JOSEPH BROWN

IT WILL BE REMEMBERED THAT during the Civil War the governor of Georgia was Joseph E. Brown (see photo on page 66). This controversial man was connected with many historical events in Georgia and Milledgeville but none quite so unusual as his "funeral," which took place in Milledgeville in late November 1864.

What was unusual about this funeral is that Governor Brown wasn't dead. In fact, he wasn't to die for thirty years. A few days before the "funeral," Governor Brown had received a telegram informing him that Union General William T. Sherman, accompanied by his army, was fast approaching Milledgeville. In the recent past, Sherman had taken Atlanta and reduced it to ashes. Governor Brown, the legislature, and many of the citizens of Milledgeville, for obvious reasons, did not want to be present when Sherman arrived. They immediately took whatever transportation was available and fled the city. Many left on foot.

It was a quiet Milledgeville that the Union army entered. No resistance was offered as the thousands of soldiers marched in. During the next days, idle army officers amused themselves by entering the State House and holding a mock session of the Georgia legislature. This minor event has become part of the folklore of Milledgeville. What has been largely forgotten is that the "session" adjourned after first passing resolutions of great sympathy and respect for "His Excellency, Governor Joseph Emerson Brown, departed." They agreed unanimously to attend, en masse, his funeral the next day and "assist in the last sad rites to be held in the Baptist church in this place." No doubt a great laugh was caused by the ironic "departed," considering it was the Union army that caused Governor Brown to hastily "depart."

The following day, several hundred Union soldiers, armed with "Joe Brown's pikes," assembled in the center of town. These pikes were medieval type weapons with a sixteen-inch blade attached to a twelve-foot staff. They had been manufactured in 1861, on Governor Brown's order, as a weapon for those soldiers for whom rifles were not available. Their only use, as far as I know, was on this one occasion.

The pikes were shipped in long boxes containing one hundred pikes. The Union soldiers emptied one of the boxes and used it as a casket. With pikes ceremoniously reversed, the soldiers marched to the solemn beat of a muffled drum as they followed officers, play-acting as they had the previous day, as members of the legislature behind the casket. This "funeral procession" wound through downtown Milledgeville before entering the Baptist church. At that time the church was located on the north side of the State House grounds.

The Baptist church was in actuality the church to which Governor Brown belonged. Several Union officers gave clever tongue-in-cheek addresses over the coffin. One man in particular, a lieutenant colonel, was clearly well up on Governor Brown's history. His address is described by Confederate officer Dr. Robert J. Massey, who was present, as a "splendid vindication of the governor's administration. No man from a southern standpoint could have done better. He was classical and cultured. His sentences well rounded and refined. He himself a logical and singularly graceful speaker."

No doubt Governor Brown heard about "his" first funeral. I suspect he was not amused. His second funeral took place after his actual death, November 30, 1894. He is buried in Oakland Cemetery in Atlanta.

# Confederate Cavalry
# Rescue Women Assaulted
# by Union Troops

IT WAS NOVEMBER 23, 1864. General William T. Sherman and his huge Union army had just arrived in Milledgeville. Dr. Robert J. Massey, the surgeon in charge of Brown Hospital, went to see General Sherman to ask for provisions, medicines and protection. Two days before, hundreds of Yankee foragers (also called "bummers") had swarmed through Milledgeville carrying away anything of value. The hospital was left without any medicine or food of any description.

General Sherman, "in a very pleasant manner," issued orders for Dr. Massey to receive whatever food or medical supplies he needed. He also issued an order providing Dr. Massey with a guard for his hospital buildings. Remarkably, these guards were instructed to take orders from Dr. Massey in preference to any Union officer.

Before Massey left Sherman's office, a courier came in and handed Sherman a dispatch. Upon reading the dispatch Sherman became angry and paced the floor. He said to Dr. Massey, "Whilst you are here, begging me for help and provisions and protection, [General Joseph] Wheeler is hovering on the outskirts of the city and murdering my men. Here is a dispatch where his men have just murdered twenty two of my men. Your man Wheeler gives me more trouble than all of Hood's army."

As all communication with the outside world had been cut off for a couple of days, Dr. Massey had no way of knowing that the Confederate cavalry was anywhere in the vicinity. He left Sherman and obtained all the provisions his hospital and hospital guards could use.

Some time later, Massey learned more about the incident about which Sherman had received the dispatch. One source was a man who had heard it secondhand from members of General Wheeler's cavalry. Another was a man who was present with the Confederate cavalry during the engagement.

It seems that a group of white and black women, perhaps twelve or more, had taken refuge in a house on the outskirts of Milledgeville. They were assaulted by a party of Yankee soldiers. Several of the women managed to escape and ran, screaming, from the house in all directions. A squad of Wheeler's cavalry was nearby and immediately went to the rescue. As Massey described it they "commenced firing upon them [the Yankees], killing them right and left, some on the beds, some under beds, some in the house, and some under the house."

In a scene that could come from a modern movie, one Union soldier ran from the house holding a woman in front of himself as protection from the Confederate gunfire. Naturally, the cavalrymen held their fire. The woman, while being used as a shield, shouted, "Shoot! Shoot! I'll suffer death that vengeance should be wreaked upon this Hessian!" A cavalryman with particularly steady hands and a lot of nerve shot "the brute" through the head, "spattering blood and brains all over this woman."

It is curious that she referred to the man as a "Hessian," a reference to the German mercenaries hired by the British during the Revolutionary War. They were noted for their violence toward civilians. Perhaps the woman was saying that he was a brute, or not an American? I suppose we'll never know.

We also may never know where this incident took place, and who the women might be. Dr. Massey does not say. The only known assault on a woman I have heard of involved Mrs. Kate Nichols, who lived across from Lockerly Hall in Midway, a mile or so south of Milledgeville. But apparently that incident did not involve a gun battle or multiple victims or assailants. I suspect the incident referred to by Dr. Massey is a separate occurrence.

# A Doctor Keeps Wartime Smallpox Cases in Milledgeville Secret for Almost Forty Years

IN THE SUMMER OF 1864, war was coming to Milledgeville. Georgia had been invaded by Union General William T. Sherman. The fighting around Atlanta had been fierce, with many casualties. Governor Brown established a hospital in Atlanta, known as Brown Hospital, for Georgia militia troops. Dr. Robert J. Massey was in charge of the hospital.

In July, Brown Hospital moved, with a hundred patients, to Milledgeville. Within weeks the hospital had several hundred patients, as each train brought more and more men to be treated. These sick and wounded were placed in six wards spread over Milledgeville in various buildings, including the male and female academies on Penitentiary Square where Georgia College & State University now stands. They were also put in tents along the south side of the square next to where the Old Courthouse now stands. Others were housed in private homes and commercial buildings on Wayne Street.

In the first part of September, Atlanta fell to Sherman. Refugees were pouring south, attempting to get out of the way of the Sherman juggernaut. Milledgeville's population of four thousand swelled with many refugees. In the midst of this bustle of humanity, one of the deadliest and most feared of all diseases appeared: smallpox.

Just the mention of the name caused panic. In its sixty years of existence, Milledgeville had several smallpox epidemics. The town would shut down; people would leave or stay indoors.

Dr. Massey was informed by an assistant physician that there was a case of smallpox in one of the hospital buildings on Wayne Street. Dr. Massey immediately went to the ward and confirmed the diagnosis. He "took but a moment to decide" on his bold and daring course of action. He quarantined the soldier with smallpox in the upstairs of the building. There were four other patients sharing the room and they were put upstairs as well. Two young women, matrons of the ward, had also been exposed, so they were put upstairs, too. Two black servants were on duty in the ward and they also were quarantined upstairs. All were immediately vaccinated.

Dr. Massey planned "to preserve most scrupulously from the outside world as a close secret the knowledge of the presence of smallpox." He would "keep the smallpox patients and every person suspected of having been exposed right in the heart of the city, quarantine them and impose upon each a solemn injunction of secrecy." He knew his assistant "to be a brave man, a man of his word, [and] could trust him in this emergency as [he] had trusted him before." He confided the plan to the assistant. He shared the secret of the plans with one other person: his own slave, a man named Matt Mitchell. He described Mitchell as "bright and intelligent" and "in every way reliable, worthy of the trust reposed in him." After being vaccinated, it was Mitchell's job to be the carrier between the infected quarters upstairs and the outside world.

The two matrons contracted smallpox. One of them was a "bad case." Despite being vaccinated, it did not take and she was "almost [a] complete sore from head to foot." However, she "safely recovered." The fate of the soldier and the others is not known.

Thirty-seven years later, in 1901, Dr. Ramsey published in an obscure newspaper this story of the 1864 smallpox outbreak in Milledgeville. He commented, "so far as I know the good people of Milledgeville to this day never knew of the existence of smallpox in the busiest part of their city." It's now been another 103 years, and "the good people of Milledgeville" are hearing of it again, or perhaps they are hearing it for the first time.

# MILLEDGEVILLE INFECTS
# SAVANNAH WITH SMALLPOX

D R. ROBERT MASSEY, THE SURGEON in charge of Brown Hospital in Milledgeville, kept secret the fact that, during the fall of 1864, smallpox had broken out at his hospital. With Sherman approaching, the Georgia legislature in session and the penitentiary and asylum housing hundreds of inmates and patients in addition to the civilian and military population, Dr. Massey thought that panic could best be avoided by keeping his smallpox patients quarantined and news of the presence of the disease under wraps.

Only a few trusted employees and slaves were aware of the smallpox contained on the third floor of a building used as a hospital in downtown Milledgeville. Despite all precautions, the Georgia legislature heard rumors that there was smallpox in the sprawling complex of buildings and tents known as Brown Hospital. They demanded that Dr. Massey provide evidence that there was no smallpox. Dr. Massey took members of the legislature on an extended tour of the many buildings. As he had hoped, the legislators were worn out by the time they got to the last building, Stetson Hall. They toured the first two floors, and when offered the opportunity to climb another set of stairs to the third floor, they declined. Had they gone up those stairs, they would have found the smallpox patients. It was a close call.

As General Sherman's army approached Milledgeville in mid-November 1864, there was only one patient left. This man was a trusted slave of Dr. Massey named Matt Mitchell. Each day, Mitchell's bedclothes would be taken out and buried or burned. When firm evidence came that Sherman was approaching Milledgeville and would arrive in a day or two, panic hit Milledgeville. People ran all over in an effort to get away. The members of the legislature fled, along with the governor and many citizens. Dr. Massey stayed to continue to care for the patients in his hospital.

Before Sherman's army arrived, a swarm of foragers, or bummers, swept through Milledgeville, taking anything of value and much of no value. There followed several tense days of Union occupation and, after their departure, the grim task of surviving on what little remained.

A few weeks after leaving Milledgeville, the Union army was in Savannah. Smallpox broke out there. But that was neither of concern to the people of Milledgeville nor to Dr. Massey. They were occupied with problems at home in Milledgeville.

Twenty years passed. Dr. Massey was now in charge of a sailors' hospital on St. Simon's Island. One day a group of sick black sailors was brought in. One man, heavily scarred by smallpox, looked familiar, but Dr. Massey could not place him. After several days, the man spoke to Dr. Massey and identified himself as Harkless, his former slave and attendant at Brown Hospital in Milledgeville. Dr. Massey had given his watch to Harkless upon Sherman's approach in hopes that it would be safe with him. The evening before the Union troops left Milledgeville, Dr. Massey was awakened in the middle of the night by a tapping at his window. Harkless was there to tell where the watch was hidden and to say that he had joined the Union army and was leaving town. Dr. Massey never expected to see Harkless again.

As they talked in the hospital at St. Simons, Harkless told Dr. Massey some things he had not known about the days of Sherman's occupation. In the excitement of the moment, the bedclothes of the smallpox patient Matt Mitchell had not been burned or buried as was the usual practice. Further, when the bummers showed up they took the blankets and sheets with them, despite Harkless's protests that they were infected. The infected bedclothes were then given out to blacks who had joined the Union army. By the time those people had gotten as far as Savannah, they had come down with smallpox, which readily spread to others.

Clearly, the smallpox that swept through the army in Savannah originated with the infected bedclothes of the patient Matt Mitchell of Brown Hospital in Milledgeville. Harkless was soon well and on his way. Dr. Massey never saw him again. It was another twenty years before he told the story of the smallpox in Milledgeville.

# THE ENEMY'S PLANS
## AND A DOCTOR'S WORD OF HONOR

DURING THE DARK DAYS OF November 1864, when Sherman's Union army blanketed Milledgeville, many despicable acts of violence, destruction and cruelty took place. A witness to these events and a participant trying to stand up for his principles was Dr. Robert J. Massey of the Confederate army.

Dr. Massey was in charge of Brown Hospital in Milledgeville. With the approach of General Sherman, he was ordered to stay behind and surrender when others were fleeing. It was Dr. Massey's responsibility to do all that he could for the patients in his care. In the course of his duties, Dr. Massey kept his eyes and ears open.

General Sherman had provided Dr. Massey with Union troops to guard his hospital buildings and his medical stores. Each day during the occupation, Dr. Massey would go to the provost marshal's office to arrange for a new set of men to act as guards. The provost marshal's office was in Governor Brown's office in the capitol building across the hall from the state library.

On one occasion, Dr. Massey observed soldiers burning armloads of books and cutting them with knives or swords. The provost marshal, Lieutenant Colonel William H. Hawley, was also present and saw that Dr. Massey was disturbed by the scene. He told Dr. Massey that he would provide him with a guard for the library if Dr. Massey would supervise the guard. Dr. Massey gratefully accepted. Whatever books were saved from destruction survived due to Dr. Massey.

While trying to put the library back into some order, Dr. Massey found himself in the presence of, but concealed from, several Union officers, including Brigadier General Absolom Baird, who had come into the library to privately discuss important military concerns. To Dr. Massey's surprise, he overheard them talking about the army's plans.

It seems that General Sherman had intended on going to Augusta and then on to Columbia, South Carolina. The idea was to get behind General Lee, who was then in Virginia protecting Richmond.

The latest news, which the officers were discussing, was a report that Confederate General Braxton Bragg was in Augusta with twenty to twenty-five thousand troops. Apparently General Sherman was quite upset by this information. Dr. Massey, not wanting to be thought to be eavesdropping, started whistling. General Baird came into view and asked if he had overheard what was being discussed. Dr. Massey replied that he had heard every word. The officers then escorted Dr. Massey to General Sherman's headquarters.

General Sherman, upon hearing the story, forcefully reprimanded his officers. Then, in a pleasant tone, he told Dr. Massey, "You will have to go with me. You are in possession of my secret, and I can't let you go till I get out of Georgia." Dr. Massey, thinking fast, replied that he was a non-combatant and that the men in his hospital would suffer if he were taken away. To this Sherman replied that he was right and he would not be required to leave Milledgeville. However, Dr. Massey would be asked to sign a parole "agreeing not to divulge anything you have seen or heard connected with my army since I have been in Milledgeville." Dr. Massey gladly signed the parole.

Four days after Sherman left Milledgeville, a Confederate sergeant and a squad of men appeared in Dr. Massey's office. Dr. Massey was a prisoner by order of General Braxton Bragg. It seems that rumors had reached General Bragg that Dr. Massey was in possession of valuable information regarding the movements of Sherman's army. General Bragg ordered Dr. Massey detained and brought to Augusta to tell him what he knew.

Dr. Massey showed him the parole he had signed promising to divulge nothing. General Bragg read it carefully, scrutinized it closely, then said: "Sir, preserve sacredly this oath. Be a soldier and solemnly observe a soldier's oath. Never divulge it till Sherman is out of Georgia." He then dismissed Dr. Massey to return to Milledgeville.

Despite the grim realities of war, there were these two bright spots: General Sherman trusting Dr. Massey's word of honor and General Bragg not asking Dr. Massey to violate his parole.

# Brigadier General Bryan M. Thomas, CSA, Milledgeville's Forgotten General

WHEN ONE THINKS OF A Confederate general from Milledgeville, the name of George Doles immediately comes to mind. If one is really interested in local trivia, the name of John W.A. Sanford may also be remembered. However, Sanford's commission was in the Georgia militia many years before the Confederacy.

Milledgeville can boast another man who became a general in the Confederate army. Bryan Morel Thomas, however, is almost forgotten in the story of Milledgeville. Perhaps he has not been remembered as he isn't buried in Milledgeville. It helps to have a tombstone to remind later generations of those in the past.

Bryan Thomas was born May 8, 1836, in Midway, a son of John Sherrod Thomas. John Sherrod Thomas was a veteran of the War of 1812 and a distinguished Baldwin County citizen. Bryan Thomas grew up in Midway and attended Oglethorpe University. He was appointed to West Point, where he graduated in 1858. As a second lieutenant in the Eighth U.S. Infantry, and later the Fifth U.S. Infantry, he was stationed on the frontier in Utah and New Mexico where he saw action against the Indians. Later he was transferred to West Point as an instructor. He resigned from the U.S. Army in April 1861 and accepted a commission as first lieutenant in the Confederate army.

He was on the staff of General Jones M. Withers at the battle of Shiloh in 1862 and, late in the year, at the battle of Murfreesboro. In August 1864, at the age of twenty-eight, he was promoted to brigadier general. He was transferred to the Department of the Gulf where he commanded a brigade of Alabama cavalry, artillery and infantry. The spring of 1865 found him at Fort Blakely, defending the city of Mobile.

Fort Blakely was a three-mile-long earthwork connecting nine batteries of artillery. Late in the afternoon of April 9, 1865, just hours after General Lee surrendered the Army of Northern Virginia, Fort Blakely's garrison of four thousand was overrun by sixteen thousand Union troops. Bryan Thomas was captured.

With the war over, Bryan Thomas turned his talents to education and farming. He farmed land in Dooly County but also became involved in higher education. After the war, he and his wife lived in part of the old Oglethorpe building in Midway where they also taught school.

In the 1880s, Thomas was offered the position of superintendent of the public schools of Dalton, Georgia. He held that position until his death, of peritonitis, in July of 1905. He was a member of the Episcopal Church in Milledgeville as a young man and in Dalton later in life. He is buried in West Hill Cemetery in Dalton. The United Daughters of the Confederacy chapter in Dalton is named for him.

# The Final Resting Place
## of Edwin Jemison

M̲y̲ ̲w̲i̲f̲e̲ ̲S̲u̲e̲ ̲a̲n̲d̲ I spend a lot of time working with cemeteries. We have photographed, indexed and researched them. Sue is the creator and webmaster of the Baldwin, Hancock and Jones Counties cemetery website, which brings us frequent inquiries from all over the world about the cemeteries and the people in them.

In the early fall of 2001, we received an inquiry from a woman in New York City. Sue forwarded it to me as I handle most of the historical questions. The woman wanted an opinion as to whether or not Edwin F. Jemison, the Confederate soldier with the famous photograph (see photo on page 65), was actually buried in Memory Hill. I replied to the inquiry saying I didn't think that he was buried there, despite that his name is on a gravestone. I suspected that he was buried at Malvern Hill, in Virginia, where he was killed in 1862. However, I did not have any proof.

That exchange of emails was the start of a flood of correspondence between us. I discovered that this woman is a historian named Alexandra Filipowski who had studied the prominent families of Milledgeville in astonishing detail. She knew not only their genealogies but their business relationships and property ownership for generations all over central Georgia.

We decided that it would be worthwhile to determine just where Jemison was buried, if we could. Even though Jemison was only a private in a Louisiana regiment, we thought that as he was the grandson of Milledgeville's prominent Baradell Stubbs, he might have been given an obituary in the Milledgeville newspapers. I went to the library and started looking in the old newspapers on microfilm. Within fifteen minutes I had a copy of his obituary in hand. The obituary says, in part, "May He who maketh wars to cease, comfort the sorrowing parents whose boy lies, buried by loving hands, on the battle field near Richmond," making it clear that, at the time of his death in 1862, he was buried with other fallen soldiers. I phoned Alexa at her office in New York with this exciting news and read the obituary to her.

I then went down to Memory Hill Cemetery and analyzed the lot where Jemison's monument stands. There was space for Jemison to be buried there in 1862. However, if he had been buried there, then there would not have been room for all the people who are now buried on that lot. There simply is not enough space. This was another clue that Jemison is not buried in Memory Hill.

Alexa and I looked into the possibility of the body being returned to Milledgeville for burial after the war, but determined that it was not brought back. Those rare cases always received newspaper coverage and we could find none. We decided that as Edwin Jemison is a name known everywhere, we would write a magazine article on his burial. We wrote the article together, passing revised and re-revised versions of it back and forth by email until we had an article with which we were satisfied. We then sent it to a magazine for publication.

Alexa's interest in Milledgeville led me to doing the unthinkable. I invited my co-author, a woman I had never met, to visit Sue and me. I should hasten to point out that I had Sue's approval. Alexa then did the unthinkable: she accepted.

She visited us in April 2002. I was continually amazed at the knowledge she has of Milledgeville and the people who lived here in the nineteenth century. She was charming and enthusiastic as we went about doing research and visiting places she had located; I was totally unaware that most of these places even existed. We drove all over central Georgia, visiting in homes and inspecting ruins of foundations of homes where prominent people connected with Milledgeville had once lived. We visited with wonderful people both in Milledgeville and elsewhere who invited us into their homes and shared history with us. Alexa took copious notes and also tape recorded interviews.

On April 26, we went to Memory Hill for Confederate Memorial Day. To our utter astonishment, a memorial to Edwin Jemison was unveiled. To our way of thinking, this memorial to the memory of Edwin Jemison is a great idea. Thomas Jefferson has a wonderful memorial in Washington, D.C., yet he's not buried there; he's buried at Monticello. Same for Edwin Jemison; he's not buried in Memory Hill, he's at Malvern Hill. People will remember Jemison for a long time; his photograph is responsible for that. It may be that Private Edwin Jemison is the only private in either army who has a monument in his honor.

I have often witnessed people coming here and standing before that monument for a moment of silence, thought or prayer for a man whom many consider represents the soldiers of the Confederacy. I would suspect that those standing by that monument find that it is a place to focus on remembrance and mourning for those who died in all wars and are buried in this cemetary and everywhere else far from home. It might be that those like Edwin Jemison, who lie in unmarked graves, are also remembered.

The article my friend Alexa Filipowski and I wrote, "Where Does Private Edwin Jemison Rest?," is published in the May 2004 issue of *America's Civil War*.

Private Edwin F. Jemison, second Louisiana Volunteer Infantry. *Courtesy Library of Congress.*

The State House. *Courtesy Special Collections, GCSU Library.*

General George P. Doles. *Courtesy Special Collections, GCSU Library.*

Governor Joseph E. Brown. *Courtesy The Old Governor's Mansion.*

ARSENAL AT MILLEDGEVILLE, DESTROYED NOVEMBER 14, 1864

The State Arsenal in 1864. *Courtesy Special Collections, GCSU Library.*

The executive mansion was the residence of Governor Brown. *Courtesy The Old Governor's Mansion.*

Union troops raising the American flag over the State House. This image originally appeared in the January 7, 1865 issue of *Harper's Weekly*. *Courtesy Special Collections, GCSU Library.*

The State Penitentiary building was set afire by Union troops in 1864. *Courtesy Special Collections, GCSU Library.*

# HELEN DORTCH LONGSTREET: THE WIFE OF GENERAL JAMES LONGSTREET

WHEN ONE FIRST HEARS OF the wife, or widow, of General James Longstreet of the Confederate army, the assumption is often that she must be someone from the distant past. Surely she belongs with the history of the Civil War and the nineteenth century.

However, the remarkable Helen Dortch Longstreet does not fit that mold. Her past is not only connected with the Civil War but also half of the twentieth century. She also has a connection with Baldwin County.

She was born in 1863 at the time that her future husband, Lieutenant General James Longstreet, was one of Robert E. Lee's top commanders. A few months after her birth, General Longstreet opposed Lee's plans at Gettysburg. For many, he has been considered "the man who lost the battle that lost the Civil War." It was a curse that was to follow him to the grave and is still debated today.

Helen Dortch met General Longstreet when she was attending Brenau College in Gainesville, Georgia in the 1880s. He was the father of her roommate. At that time Longstreet was married to his first wife, Louisa. Louisa died in 1889. Helen married General Longstreet at the governor's mansion in Atlanta in 1897. She was thirty-four; he was seventy-six.

In 1893 and 1894 she was the editor of the populist newspaper *The Milledgeville Chronicle*. She was active in women's suffrage, civil rights and the establishment of Georgia Normal and Industrial College, now Georgia College & State University, here in Milledgeville.

In 1894, Helen Dortch was appointed assistant state librarian, making her the first woman to hold public office in the Georgia state government. Two years later she authored the "Dortch Bill," allowing women to hold the office of state librarian, which was passed by the Georgia legislature.

After her marriage to General Longstreet, she fought continuously to rehabilitate his military reputation. This became a lifetime project that went on into the 1950s. As part of this effort, she wrote two biographies of Longstreet and organized the Longstreet Memorial Association. She lectured frequently on the Civil War. In 1939, she arranged for the Longstreet Memorial Exhibit at the New York World's Fair in 1939 and in 1940 at the Golden Gate Exposition in San Francisco. She worked for half a century to get a statue and monument to "the General," as she called her husband, at Gettysburg.

After General Longstreet died in 1904, she was appointed postmistress of the Gainesville Post Office; she was the first female to hold the position in Georgia. She stayed at that job until 1913. She became active in politics. She supported Theodore Roosevelt's "Bull Moose" party in 1912 and was a delegate to the Progressive Party's National Convention. From 1911 to 1913 she fought, and lost, a battle with Georgia Power Company. She had attempted to prevent the building of the power dam at Tallulah Falls for environmental reasons. Today at Tallulah Gorge State Park the trails are named the "Helen Dortch Longstreet Trail System" in her honor.

In 1943, at the age of eighty, this feisty lady obtained a job at the Bell Aircraft Corporation's bomber plant in Marietta. She learned to be a riveter and assembler of B-29 bombers. She was outspoken against the labor union, which she refused to join, saying, "I do not believe a union had a place in a war plant during time of war…I am an American and entitled to my opinions and the right to express them as I may." The union considered her a "real old lady" and tried to get her out of the plant. She refused to give her age or to resign and concentrated on her work, saying, "Never mind my age, I can handle that riveting thing as well as anyone. I'm intending to complete in five weeks three courses which normally take three months to finish." She did, too. The union claimed she was hired by Bell Aircraft only for publicity.

She got a great deal of publicity. Newspapers across the country carried articles about the widow of General Longstreet fighting on the home front in World War II. *Life* magazine carried an article with photographs of the determined gray-haired lady operating a riveter and assembling aircraft. She was at the plant for two years and never missed a day at work or came in late. She said that World War II was "the most horrible war of them all. It makes General Sherman look like a piker. I want to get it over with. I want to build bombers to bomb Hitler." A foreman described her work as ranking with the best in the plant. When not working, she would faithfully answer the hundreds of letters she received supporting her efforts.

In 1947, she spoke to a Georgia legislative committee in Atlanta to denounce the Herman Talmadge white primary bill, which allowed only whites to vote in the primary, as "monstrous" and "infamous." When she was finished, she received a standing ovation from the committeemen. In 1950, she announced her candidacy for governor of Georgia. She said, "It is conceded that Governor Talmadge cannot be defeated by anyone in sight. I feel the obligation now falls on Georgia's women to furnish the type of governor the state deserves." She lost the election but she had made her point and spoken her mind.

With the Korean War looming in 1950, Helen Dortch Longstreet offered to go back into the bomber factory as part of the war effort, saying, "I'll have you know I'm no lowly riveter. I'm an assembler, although I sometimes filled in as a riveter in emergencies." The plant, however, did not reopen, so her offer was not taken.

In the spring of 1956, her life took a downward turn. After taking a bus in upstate New York, she was found wandering and incoherent in the city of Elmira. Relatives were located in Georgia to care for her. In 1957, she was placed in Central State Hospital in Milledgeville. She died May 3, 1962, at the age of ninety-nine, and was buried in West View Cemetery in Atlanta.

# THE LOST FLAG OF
# THE FOURTH GEORGIA REGIMENT

IN APRIL OF 1861, A local militia company, the Baldwin Blues, marched off to war. They were incorporated into the Confederate army as Company H, Fourth Georgia Volunteer Infantry. At their head was Milledgeville native, Captain George P. Doles (see photo on page 66).

Doles was soon elected colonel of the regiment. He served with conspicuous bravery and gallantry in the great battles of Virginia and Maryland. After the battle of Sharpsburg in 1862, he was promoted to brigadier general. He served in that position until his death.

General Doles was killed at the battle of Cold Harbor on June 2, 1864. His body was returned to Milledgeville for a huge state funeral. His remains lay in state with his sword, captured enemy flags and a myrtle wreath on his coffin. Of particular interest to us is the "bullet torn battle flag of the Fourth Georgia Regiment" which stood in the place of honor at the head of the casket.

After the service and the burial ceremony at Memory Hill, the Fourth Georgia Flag was presented to Sarah Doles, his widow.

Two years later, General Sherman's huge army was approaching Milledgeville on his march to the sea. Nothing was safe. People were hiding everything of value as best they could. Everything had to be hidden, from whiskey to jewelry to silverware; even the old battle worn flag of the Fourth Georgia. It was common practice to bury valuables and hope that no one gave away the location of the treasure.

Mrs. Doles had a different idea. She hid her precious flag under the loose coping bricks of a local well. At that time there were public wells in many places in Milledgeville. This wasn't as bold as "hiding" the flag in "plain sight" but it was pretty close. The wells would be frequented by many local people and thousands of Federal soldiers. The flag would literally be right under their hands.

The hiding place proved to be successful. The flag was not discovered and after the enemy army left town Mrs. Doles retrieved it. She kept the flag for the next twenty-five years. In 1889, when Mrs. Doles was dying, she entrusted the flag to James F. Murphy.

Murphy had been an ensign in the Fourth Georgia Regiment and had carried the flag during the war. In 1891, Murphy decided that he would present the flag to the governor of Georgia, William Northen, so it would remain the property of the citizens of Georgia. There is no record of the governor ever having received the flag, and the state of Georgia does not now possess the flag in its extensive flag collection.

In 1894, the huge monument marking the graves of General Doles and his wife and daughter was unveiled in Memory Hill Cemetery. The occasion was a reunion of the Fourth Georgia and was well attended by surviving veterans. Accounts of the festivities and ceremonies fail to mention the old flag of the regiment.

What became of the tattered old flag that had survived battles and General Sherman's army is a mystery. Perhaps it still exists and is waiting to be rediscovered.

# SIMON WHEELER, CONFEDERATE YANKEE

THERE ARE WELL OVER THREE hundred Confederate veterans buried in Memory Hill Cemetery. Along with them are several men who fought for the Union. All of these Yankees came to make their homes in Milledgeville after the war. There is nothing unusual about that. However, the case of Simon Wheeler, formerly a Union soldier, has a unique twist.

An Indiana farmer in his early thirties, Wheeler enlisted in the Union army during the Civil War. After the war he returned to Indiana and to farming. He was a very serious farmer and belonged to several agricultural societies.

Wheeler prospered as a farmer and in the 1870s and 1880s found himself financially well off. He dabbled in politics and was elected to the Indiana state legislature. He was a staunch Democrat.

In the 1890s, this prosperous farmer, now in his mid-sixties, sold his property in Indiana and moved to Milledgeville along with his wife. He bought land in Scottsboro and began farming again. He managed his land well and was very successful. He planted the first Elberta peach orchard in Baldwin County.

He did not enter politics locally. However, he was well known as being very interested in public affairs and could discuss them intelligently. He had a wonderful sense of humor and frequently spoke at public gatherings where it was said he would effectively retain the attention of the audience. He was an honest and well-liked man.

He did something that certainly was highly unusual, if not unique. He joined George Doles's Camp no. 730, of the United Confederate Veterans, and attended the meetings. The organization was comprised of Confederate veterans of the Civil War. It says something about Wheeler that these aging Confederate veterans would admit him to their group. His views must have been very similar to those of his former enemies. They too must have seen in him a kindred spirit despite his past connection with the Union army.

In 1910, this Confederate Yankee contracted pneumonia and died at the age of seventy-nine. He was buried with Masonic honors. No doubt his Confederate veteran friends attended the funeral.

The grave of Simon Wheeler is marked with a tombstone. Soon an additional stone will be placed, which will cite his service in the Union army.

# CARLOS WILSON:
# SOLDIER, INVENTOR, BUSINESSMAN

C ARLOS WILSON WAS NOT NATIVE to Milledgeville. He was born in Poughkeepsie, New York, in 1843. While still a small child he moved with his parents to Kent County, Michigan. There, he grew to manhood.

He enlisted in the Union army at the age of nineteen on September 2, 1861. He was a bugler in Company F, Second Michigan Cavalry. He served until October 2, 1864, when he was discharged at Nashville, Tennessee. He never came to Milledgeville as a soldier.

Shortly after the war, however, he came to Milledgeville. About 1870, he married a woman from Georgia and started to raise a family. He owned Wilson's grocery store. He was also an inventor. In 1872, he was granted a patent on a Cotton Seed Planter & Guano Distributing machine.

In late 1874, he sold his store to his brother, Horace Wilson, and to Peter Meadows. Carlos leased the McComb Hotel where he was proprietor.

As he had sold the store, he was not present in December 1874, when his brother Horace got into an argument with thirty-two-year-old Frederick McComb in the barroom of the grocery store. Hot words were followed by gunshots from both Horace Wilson and Peter Meadows as they fired at Fred McComb. McComb, who had been wounded at Spotsylvania as a member of Company H, Fourth Georgia Infantry, died almost instantly with a bullet in his chest.

The bullet was removed from McComb, and it matched the caliber of the pistol used by Horace Wilson. At the trial, Peter Meadows was acquitted. Horace Wilson, veteran of the Tenth Michigan Infantry, was sentenced to four years in the penitentiary for voluntary manslaughter. Horace was not a prisoner long. Before he could be transferred to the penitentiary, a mob of his friends, in the middle of the night, forced the jailor to release him. Horace fled to Michigan where he lived a productive life.

Carlos Wilson had another brother, Merritt Wilson. Merritt was in the Third Michigan Infantry during the Civil War. He was visiting Carlos in the summer of 1880 when he fell over dead of unknown causes at the age of thirty-five. Merritt is buried in Memory Hill Cemetery.

In the late 1870s, Carlos became the postmaster of Milledgeville. This occupation apparently did not consume all of his time or energy, as he kept trying to invent useful machines. In 1888, he invented a cotton press. At that time cotton was compressed into bales of various sizes and weights. When these bales were shipped to Liverpool, England, the shipping costs were higher than they would have been if all bales were the same size and packed very densely. Wilson's cotton press would solve that problem. He received widespread attention for his innovative design and was granted a patent for his press in 1893.

Despite having been a bugler during the Civil War, Carlos was a crack shot with a rifle. In 1886, he was on the Milledgeville Rifle Team where he easily was the best marksman. No doubt the Union veteran and his friends, many of them Confederate veterans, had some good times during their rifle competitions.

Wilson's life took a downward twist in 1901. He was arrested and taken to jail in Macon by Federal marshals. Apparently Wilson was speculating in cotton futures and using post office funds to do it. He would always replace the money so the post office was never short. However, it was in violation of the law. The amount of money in question was $680. Wilson was permanently removed from his position as postmaster.

Carlos Wilson died in 1906 while on a visit to a son in Atlanta. He was buried in Memory Hill with full Masonic honors. On April 30, 2005, as part of the Confederate Memorial Day ceremony, the United Daughters of the Confederacy and the Sons of Confederate Veterans unveiled a new tombstone at his grave. Confederate reenactors saluted this former Union soldier.

# WOMEN RIOT IN MILLEDGEVILLE

W HEN WE THINK OF THE Civil War we think of Gettysburg, Sharpsburg, Manassas or any of hundreds of battles and skirmishes. However, there was more going on during the war than combat. On the home front there were very tough times as well.

Those left behind, the women and children, as well as the old men and boys, were faced with a battle of their own. I'm talking about the economic battle of trying to find enough money to acquire the food and necessities to maintain life. We have all heard about the high inflation and the scarcity of various products and food.

I doubt, however, that we have a good idea as to just how desperate the economics were. In our own recent past, we have seen inflation at extremely low levels—on the order of less than 2 or 3 percent per year. Twenty years ago, the inflation rate was over 10 percent per year: "double digit" inflation. People were screaming that it was a nightmare.

Recent inflation rates are a mere trifle when compared to the inflation rates in the 1860s in the Confederacy. In 1861, the first year of the war, the Confederacy did well on the battlefield. By September the price index was up "only" 25 percent for the year. However, by the end of the year it was up over 50 percent.

The Confederacy did not fare as well on the battlefield in the spring of 1862. This pushed the price index up 100 percent in the first half of 1862. Incredibly, it jumped another 100 percent the second half of the year. Wage rates rose about 55 percent in 1862, while prices rose 300 percent. At the beginning of 1863, it took seven dollars to buy what a dollar had bought two years earlier.

Scapegoats were eagerly sought to blame for the economic disaster. The merchants were easy targets. Many were accused of being "speculators" or "extortioners." The newspaper, the *Richmond* [Virginia] *Examiner* said that "the whole South stinks with the lust of extortion."

But the reality was that few merchants actually did speculate in food or merchandise. They may have marked up their goods by 50 percent, but when inflation was running at 10 or 15 percent per month, they made little profit in real net dollars.

Desperate citizens appealed for help to their local and state governments as well as to the Confederate government in Richmond. Unfortunately, there was no help for the situation. The Confederacy's economy was based on agriculture and simply could not finance a war and produce consumer goods of any sort at the same time. Therefore, the economy collapsed and nothing was produced in adequate quantities.

Cities all over the South began to experience food riots. Usually, these riots were caused by women desperate to feed their families while their men were in the military. The riots were similar in most cases. A mob of angry women, some armed with knives or revolvers, would march to a store or warehouse and demand food or other commodities. There was really no way to stop the mob and the premises would be looted.

In April 1864, this happened in Milledgeville. Three hundred angry women, many of them "well clothed" and some even "elegantly clad," stormed the dry goods store of Charles W. Gause. They took what they wanted. Apparently, they did this without actual violence, although their number and demeanor would certainly have been threatening.

Facing the angry mob, Judge Iverson Louis Harris of the Supreme Court made an "eloquent" appeal to the women, and they dispersed without violence or looting other stores. They did, however, take their spoils of war with them. It was said that they "didn't want anything but the fine things."

The local newspapers did not carry the story. The names of these three hundred women are unknown. It should be remembered that three hundred women represented a huge percentage of the adult female population of Milledgeville. Undoubtedly, many prominent women we remember today participated in the riot at Gause's dry goods store.

# THE FORGOTTEN CONFEDERATE SOLDIERS OF BROWN HOSPITAL

I N 1868, THE LADIES OF Milledgeville erected a monument in what is now Memory Hill Cemetery. The monument was built to commemorate the Confederate dead, wherever they may be buried. The monument was placed in the lot where non-local Confederate soldiers, hospitalized in Brown Hospital after being wounded or becoming sick in the Atlanta campaign, had been buried in 1864. Those men, whose identities were known in 1864, were by 1868 unknown. The monument bears the inscription "To Our Unknown Confederate Dead."

Every year, for generations, veterans, war widows, sons and daughters of veterans, and their grandchildren and great grandchildren have come to this monument to pay homage to the Confederate soldiers and to the men who died in the hospital. It never occurred to anyone that the identities of the unknown soldiers would or could be found.

In the early spring of 2003, a remarkable event took place that changed the history of the monument. I was reading the *Southern Recorder* newspaper of September 13, 1864, in the Georgia College & State University library. I was not looking for unknown soldiers. I literally sucked in my breath when I saw a short article entitled "List of persons who have died at Brown Hospital since its establishment, to 10th of September." A list of names followed along with the death dates. I read it over again. And again. I had not read it wrong. These men had died in Brown Hospital. One name stood out from the others: "J.N. Meadows." I knew that name, or a variation of it, as one that was on a Veterans Administration marker next to the Confederate monument.

I quickly dropped a dime into the slot and made a copy of the page. I made two copies, to be safe. I quickly looked around the library and did not see anyone I could share this information with who would understand the emotions running through me.

I left the library and headed for the cemetery. In a few minutes, I was standing alone next to the Confederate monument: I was the only person on the face of the earth, or in the past 139 years, who knew the names of the men buried here. I stood there for quite awhile.

The problem now was one of what to do with this information. Clearly, these men must have a monument. I went to see my friend Louise Horne as she was a longtime member of the United Daughters of the Confederacy and would know what to do. When I told her I knew who the unknown soldiers were, she almost leaped out of her chair as she exclaimed, "That's the biggest thing to ever happen!" I gave her a copy of the article. She fully shared my excitement.

As time went on, the Sons of Confederate Veterans and the United Daughters of the Confederacy wanted individual Veterans Administration markers, as well as a single monument to explain who the men were and how they came to be buried here. Money was raised by both organizations as well as interested individuals.

I spent a great deal of time combing the newspapers looking for other information about Brown Hospital and the men who died there. There wasn't a lot to find. Only occasionally would a man be mentioned in the paper as having died in the hospital. The hospital itself was named for Governor Joseph Brown and had been moved from Atlanta in July to avoid the onslaught of Sherman's army. The hospital was for the exclusive use of the Georgia militia. The hospital was not in one location in Milledgeville. Wards were established in the male and female academies on the southwest corner of the square where Georgia College & State University now stands. In 1864, the prison had stood on this square. Brown Hospital soon outgrew those buildings and spread across the south side of the square in tents to where the old courthouse now stands. Brown Hospital also had wards in local hotels and some patients in private homes.

To get Veterans Administration markers for the men, I would have to find official Confederate or Georgia records giving their full names and units to verify their service. From what I'd been able to gather so far, I had surnames but only a few first names and just initials for the rest of the men. I also only had unit information for a few of the soldiers.

I started to track the doctor in charge of the hospital, Robert J. Massey. To my delight, I found that in about 1900 he wrote a series of history articles for the *Atlanta Constitution*. Some of his articles were about his time when he was associated with Brown Hospital in Milledgeville. In one of the articles he said that he wrote out daily reports and sent them to his boss, Samuel Hollingsworth Stout, who was in charge of the hospitals of the Army of Tennessee. I wondered if those records could possibly have survived. Far more likely they were used in fires to warm hands during the winter of 1865 when the war was all but over.

To my astonishment, I found that a huge collection of Dr. Stout's papers were at the University of Texas at Austin. I wrote the library there a very polite inquiry stating that

I was interested in the records for the hospital in Milledgeville. I asked if I could hire a graduate student who would be willing to go through the papers for me and make copies. A week later, a big envelope arrived from the University of Texas at Austin library. Inside I found a modest bill for copying costs and copies of the hospital records written by Dr. Massey in 1864. I spread them out on the floor and went through them page by page. Here were my men. In almost every case, I now had a full name and military unit as well as a death date. The markers from the Veterans Administration as well as a new monument could now be ordered. As an added bonus the university had also sent me the information from Stout Hospital in Midway, two miles away. The men who died there are in unmarked graves in Old Midway Cemetery. It was decided to include them on the new bronze marker with the men from Brown Hospital.

On April 26, 2004, the markers and monument were dedicated. Volleys were fired over the graves of the soldiers. Their names and units were called out as red roses were placed in front of their markers. The Confederate soldiers from Brown Hospital were no longer forgotten.

The following is the wording on the new monument:

*The Unknown Soldiers of Brown Hospital*

*These Confederate soldiers, all serving in the Georgia militia, died at Brown Hospital in Milledgeville and were buried at this location. Their names soon became lost and they were considered Unknown Soldiers until 2003 when their identities were discovered.*

*Marion Adkinson, Pvt., Co. F, 5ᵗʰ Regt., August 23, 1864*

*James T. Buckner, Pvt., Co. F, 9ᵗʰ Regt., August 31, 1864*

*Hugh Cannell, Pvt., Co. E, 12ᵗʰ Regt., September 3, 1864*

*Elisha B. Cape, Pvt., Co. A, 5ᵗʰ Regt., August 29, 1864*

*Edward M. Clark, Pvt., Co. F, 1ˢᵗ Bn., September 1, 1864*

*Ringold Commander, Pvt., Co. B, G.M.I. Cadet, August 27, 1864*

*J.R. Ellis, Co. B, 2ⁿᵈ Bn., August 4, 1864*

*William Fussell, Pvt., Co. B, 2ⁿᵈ Regt., August 29, 1864*

*James M. Green, Pvt., Co. F, 9ᵗʰ Regt., August 31, 1864*

*Willis Harrell, Pvt., Co. I, 2ⁿᵈ Regt., September 7, 1864*

*J.M. Hutcherson, Pvt., Co. K, 6ᵗʰ Regt., August 24, 1864*

*William E. Joyner, Pvt., Co. F, 8ᵗʰ Regt., September 7, 1864*

*Thomas Judge, Pvt., Co. G, 2ⁿᵈ Regt., August 24, 1864*

*John N. Meadors, Pvt., Co. D, 1ˢᵗ Regt., July 28, 1864*

*Roland Mercer, Pvt., Co. F, 7ᵗʰ Regt., September 10, 1864*

*Owen Ramsey, Pvt., Co. I, 5ᵗʰ Regt., August 16, 1864*

*Aaron Rogers, Pvt., Co. C, 2ⁿᵈ Regt., August 22, 1864*
*William Tapley, Pvt., Co. H, 2ⁿᵈ Regt., September 3, 1864*
*Reddick Thornton, Pvt., Co. I, 11ᵗʰ Regt., August 27, 1864*
*William Tillory, Pvt., Co. D, 1ˢᵗ Regt., September 12, 1864*
*Green B. Turner, Pvt., Co. F, 6ᵗʰ Regt., August 18, 1864*
*J.M. Winn, Co. F, 2ⁿᵈ Regt., August 2, 1864*
*Mordicai W. Wood, Pvt., Co. I, 1ˢᵗ Regt., August 23, 1864*
*James J. Wren, Pvt., Co. G, 2ⁿᵈ Regt., September 8, 1864*

*The following Confederate soldiers died at Stout Hospital in Midway, Ga. They are buried at Midway Cemetery in unmarked graves.*

*William R. Etheridge, Pvt., Co. K, 57ᵗʰ Georgia, August 1, 1864*
*Frank Marion Herndon, Pvt., Phelan's Battery, September 17, 1864*
*Frank Washington Legare, Pvt., Co. E, 5ᵗʰ Georgia Militia, September 27, 1864*
*John Lemmons, Pvt., Co. H, 24ᵗʰ South Carolina, March 13, 1865*
*Henry Walker, Pvt., Co. E, 1ˢᵗ & 4ᵗʰ Missouri, July 30, 1864*

# "For Want of a Nail..."

FOR WANT OF A NAIL, the shoe was lost; for want of a shoe the horse was lost; and for want of a horse the rider was lost, being overtaken and slain by the enemy, all for want of care about a horseshoe nail." This quotation from Benjamin Franklin's "Poor Richard's Almanack," of June 1758, is a gentle reminder that major consequences may stem from very small beginnings.

Indulging in the "what ifs" of history is seldom time well spent. To speculate on such things as what would have happened "if" such and such had, or had not, taken place, setting in motion a chain of events with an entirely different historical outcome, is far too time-consuming for me. Also, since it did not happen, there doesn't seem to be much point in the exercise.

However, there was a minor event in Milledgeville's past that could, or might, have had a tremendous impact on American history. Anne Buckner Burgamy, a Civil War historian, acquainted me with a fascinating connection that Milledgeville, Georgia, has with Colonel Joshua Lawrence Chamberlain.

Colonel Joshua Lawrence Chamberlain is best known as the charismatic leader of the Twentieth Maine Regiment in the Civil War. In particular, his eternal fame was secured at the battle of Gettysburg. Chamberlain was not a professional soldier. He was a professor at Bowdoin College who joined the army in 1862. At a critical moment in the battle of Gettysburg, it was discovered that a low hill, Little Round Top, at the extreme end of the Union line, was unmanned. This position was absolutely critical because if the Confederate forces had been able to place artillery on this hill, the entire Union army would be under their guns. Possession of Little Round Top would also allow the Confederates to get behind the Union lines where not only would they likely defeat the Union army but they would also be placing themselves between the Union army and Washington, D.C. The battle of Gettysburg, and perhaps the war itself, was at stake.

Chamberlain was ordered to take his men to Little Round Top and hold it. Chamberlain and his 308 officers and men of the Twentieth Maine ran to the top of the hill at the same time that Confederate units were also coming up the hill from the other side. Fighting was fierce; at times it was hand to hand. For two hours, Chamberlain withstood repeated attacks from several Confederate regiments. Finally, with a third of his men killed or wounded and the survivors out of ammunition, it appeared that Chamberlain could defend the hill no longer. The hill, and victory, was within the grasp of the Confederacy. Chamberlain ordered his men to fix bayonets on their empty rifles and to charge down the slopes of Little Round Top into the Confederates who were forming for another assault. Large numbers of Confederates, taken by surprise, surrendered; the rest retreated. Little Round Top was safe in the hands of the Union army.

Chamberlain did not know it, but the Confederate government was contemplating offering a negotiated peace with the United States if Gettysburg was a Confederate victory. As Confederate Colonel William C. Oates, who opposed Chamberlain at the fight at Little Round Top, said, Chamberlain's "skill and persistency and the great bravery of his men saved Little Round Top and the Army of the Potomac from defeat. Great events sometimes turn on comparatively small affairs."

In 1852, a twenty-seven-year-old lady appeared in Milledgeville. She was Frances "Fannie" Adams of New England. This well-educated woman was to be a music teacher at The Milledgeville Female Academy, which was located on the southwest corner of the square where Georgia College & State University is now located. She was also to give piano lessons and play the organ at the Presbyterian Church. When she first came to Milledgeville, she lived with her distant relation, Mrs. Abby Orme, the wife of Richard M. Orme, at 251 South Liberty Street. Later, she moved to the home of Samuel Gore White, which was on South Jefferson Street. It was torn down in 1958. She also lived for a time at the home of Dr. Augustus Parke Williams, which still stands on the southeast corner of South Liberty Street and Washington Street. She stayed in Milledgeville for three years. During that time she kept in touch with her fiancé who was studying for the ministry at Bangor Theological Seminary. Her fiancé was Joshua Lawrence Chamberlain.

The couple exchanged many letters while Fannie was in Milledgeville. In those letters we read that Chamberlain was seriously considering leaving the seminary and becoming a professor at the University of Georgia. As it happened, he became a professor at Bowdoin College instead. In 1855, Fannie left Milledgeville, went to Maine and married Chamberlain.

One cannot help but think of Benjamin Franklin's quotation about the losses resulting from "want of a nail." Also, as Colonel Oates referred to Little Round Top, "great events sometimes turn on comparatively small affairs." If Chamberlain had gone to the University of Georgia, he likely would not have been the man who inspired the men of the twentieth Maine at Gettysburg. Little Round Top may have fallen, the battle of Gettysburg may have become a Confederate victory, and the Civil War may have ended with an independent Confederate States of America.

# TRAGEDY AND DISASTER
## AT GRISWOLDVILLE

Tuesday, November 22, 1864, was a grim day for Milledgeville. The past several days had been consumed in the rush to hide valuables and also to get out of town while there was yet time. Rumors of Yankees, thousands of them, were pouring in from anyone who arrived. The governor and the legislature had fled. The meager defense forces had fled. The few able-bodied men in town had mostly fled. The telegraph lines to the outside world were cut. The town was left to the women, children, old men and invalids. They remained behind shuttered windows in closed-up houses.

In the early afternoon the mayor, Boswell B. deGraffenreid, met the advance units of the Twentieth Corps and surrendered the city while begging that homes and residents be protected.

While all of Milledgeville waited expectantly for what would happen, a distant rumble, as if of thunder, was heard. But, it was not the thunder of a storm. It was the thunder of cannons and musketry. The tense people of Milledgeville did not know that what they were hearing was the battle of Griswoldville, twenty miles to the southwest. As tragic as it was to find thousands of Union troops in Milledgeville, few would die as a result. However, the disaster unfolding at Griswoldville would cost many lives in a useless slaughter.

The disaster of Griswoldville was years in the making. Governor Joseph E. Brown rewarded political friends with commissions in the Georgia militia. In addition, as the militia would, in theory, only be used on Georgia soil, it was a far safer place to be than in regular Confederate service. The officers and soldiers were exempt from the Confederate draft. After three years of war most officers and men in

Confederate service had seen combat. Some had seen a great deal of combat. This was not the case with the militia.

The citizen-soldiers of the militia not only were inexperienced but also were the butt of jokes and even songs. Frequently referred to as "Joe Brown's Pets," they were often the laughing stock of both the press and regular army soldiers. Their lowly status in the eyes of their fellow Georgians rankled many of the officers and men. Many hoped for a successful battle or two that would enhance the reputation of them and their units.

As Sherman's left wing headed for Milledgeville from the north, his right wing made a feint toward Macon and then turned east to pass through Gordon before crossing the Oconee River.

In Macon, the thinking was that the Union army was heading toward Augusta. The Georgia militia was ordered to follow the Central Railroad to Gordon and then on to Augusta. Unknown to the planners of this mission, the Georgia militia was on a collision course with the entire right wing of Sherman's army.

After a skirmish on the morning of November 22 with General Wheeler's Confederate Cavalry, Charles C. Walcutt's Second Brigade of Wood's First Division entrenched and barricaded a position along a ridgeline a mile east of Griswoldville. His total command, including cavalry and artillery, was about three thousand. Many of his men were armed with the Spencer repeating rifles that could be fired at a far faster rate than a conventional muzzle loading rifle. The Union soldiers were hardened combat veterans.

Three Georgia militia brigades, two Georgia State Line regiments, two battalions of General Cobb's Confederate Reserves plus a battery of artillery left Macon in several groups, all with the goal of reaching Augusta. The total force was roughly 2,300 men. Major General Gustavus W. Smith was to have overall command. Smith, however, remained in Macon. Apparently, even with the foe at the very doorstep of Macon, he thought he could best serve by arranging for the transportation of ammunition and supplies. In his stead, the command rested with the senior officer of the Georgia militia, Brigadier General Pleasant J. Philips.

Philips was the senior officer based on his service in the militia. However, he was the least experienced brigadier general in the Georgia militia. His only service with the Confederate army was at peaceful Savannah from November 1861 to May 1862. He was a successful banker businessman, not a soldier.

General Smith sent Philips an unclear order on the morning of November 22, shortly after the militia had left Macon, which said, "Wheeler having retired to the right, keep a close lookout with your skirmishers, and avoid a fight with a superior force. You can best judge the direction. The wagon train will not leave this evening."

Within an hour Smith sent Philips a second order. "If pressed by a superior force, fall back upon this place [Macon] without bringing on a serious engagement if you can do so. If not, fall back upon the road indicated in General Toombs' note."

By the time this second order reached Philips he apparently had already decided to commence a battle. He had been moving eastward along the railroad when he came upon two militia units drawn up in line of battle. They had just made contact with the Union pickets of Walcutt's brigade. For some unknown reason, Philips made the decision to attack the Union force behind those pickets without knowing its strength.

The field of battle was entirely in favor of the Union defenders, who were protected by their entrenchments and barricades. An open field six hundred yards wide was across their front. Two hundred yards in front of the Union lines, down a slope, was a small stream running parallel with the Union lines, whose banks were covered by small trees.

Philips began the battle with his artillery. These pieces were well served by the only veterans among his troops. They did considerable damage to the Union artillery as well and probably caused most of the casualties to the Union forces that day. Their fire forced the Union artillery to withdraw.

Philips ordered his various units to charge across open ground to the small stream and then advance up the slope to the Union position. The Georgia militia crossed the stream to within fifty yards of the Union line when they found themselves being fired on from both the front and their rear. One of the other inexperienced militia units had come up behind them and thought the militia unit ahead of them was the enemy and was firing on them.

In confusion, the Georgia militia retreated to the cover of the small stream and was joined by those who had come from the rear. Crammed into the limited confines of the streambed, the fire from the Georgia militia swept over the heads of the Union defenders. The fire from the Union troops, however, was devastating to the Georgia militia.

The inexperienced Georgia militia made several attempts to overrun the Union position. The soldiers would climb out of the relative safety of the streambed and, with rebel yells and flags flying, make a rush toward the Union lines. They were repeatedly beaten back by the veteran Union troops to the streambed with heavy losses. As evening came on, the members of the Georgia militia slowly drifted off the field, leaving many of their wounded. They returned to Macon.

As the Union troops slowly crossed the field to confirm that the enemy had left, they were sickened with what they found. The ground, especially at the streambed, was covered with the dead and wounded. An officer from the 103rd Illinois Regiment described the scene: "Old grey-haired and weakly-looking men and little boys, not over 15 years old, lay dead or writhing in pain...I hope we will never have to shoot at such men again. They knew nothing at all about fighting, and I think their officers knew as little, or else, certainly knew nothing about our being there."

The Union reported its own losses to be 13 killed and 79 wounded. The Confederates reported that they had lost 51 dead and 472 wounded. These figures seem very low. Whatever the toll, it was a very grim day for the Georgia militia. The men's courage had been demonstrated, but at high cost.

The officers—in particular General Smith and General Philips—struggled to explain their actions. Why had not Smith gone with the troops instead of allowing the command to fall to the inexperienced Philips? What could Philips have been thinking when he ordered the first attack against an enemy of unknown strength? Then, after seeing the firepower he was facing, why order further attacks? Perhaps Philips was inebriated, as some reports suggest. Did it all boil down to inexperience, or was there an effort to erase the stigma of being "Joe Brown's Pets?"

Whatever the cause of the disaster was, in the end it was a useless waste of men. At the end of the day on November 22, Milledgeville, Georgia's capital, was occupied by thousands of enemy troops.

# Rufus Kelly, an Unlikely Hero

James Rufus Kelly was a private in Company B, Fourteenth Georgia Infantry. He, like many thousands of other young men, enlisted in the spring of 1861 and soon found himself in battles in Virginia. Virginia was a long way from his home in Gordon, Georgia.

In May of 1864, Rufus Kelly was struck in the leg by a bullet. As was often the case with such wounds the leg was amputated four inches above the knee. His military duties over, Rufus Kelly was discharged. He made his way back home to Gordon. The war was a distant tragic scene of which he was no longer a part.

In 1864, the war came a bit closer as General Sherman's blue-coated army fought its way to Atlanta. However, Atlanta was still a long way from Gordon. In November, the war took on a new phase, as Sherman moved his army out of Atlanta and cut a path of destruction across Georgia. Sherman split his army into two parts. The left wing went east from Atlanta and then turned south, going through Eatonton to Milledgeville. At the same time, the right wing made a move toward Macon and then turned to go east, passing south of Milledgeville. The small town of Gordon was in its path.

Each wing of Sherman's army was made up of about thirty thousand battle-hardened veterans. There was not much resistance to this huge force. Confederate General "Fighting Joe" Wheeler's cavalry of three thousand men would harass the Union army but could do little real damage. The Georgia militia was made up of old men and boys. They were at Macon.

Milledgeville was defended by a ragtag assembly of store clerks, Georgia Military Institute cadets, pardoned prisoners still wearing their striped prison uniforms and other makeshift units. In total, they numbered perhaps seven hundred. Clearly, they were in no position to make a stand. Their commander, General Henry C. Wayne, was well aware of the fighting capabilities of his little army. He wisely withdrew his forces to Gordon.

On a cold November 21, 1864, General Wayne knew he had to retreat again. This time he was going east along the railroad from Gordon to the Oconee River. He would place his men at the railroad bridge and, from that stronger defensive position, try to hold the Union army. He was waiting for a train to take his men to the river.

As he sat at Gordon's station contemplating the dim future, he was surprised to see a young man ride up on horseback. The young man was in civilian clothes and was carrying a rifle. A pair of crutches were strapped to the horse, as the man had only one leg. The young man saluted and introduced himself as Rufus Kelly. Kelly volunteered to ride to the west and watch for approaching Yankees. General Wayne told him to go ahead.

A few hours later, Kelly came dashing back to the station. The Yankees were in sight. It was just a four-man patrol he had seen approaching Gordon, but clearly more Yankees were not far behind. General Wayne, realizing that he could not stand and fight, ordered his men to board the train. Kelly was outraged. He spewed forth a volley of profanity and declared that he would defend Gordon. He would do it by himself if necessary. He turned his horse to the west and was about to gallop off when he was joined by another man, John R. Bragg.

The two men rode off into the west. They got just beyond Gordon when they saw the four horsemen. Kelly and Bragg fired. Two Union soldiers fell from their mounts. The two remaining enemy cavalrymen fled the field.

The main body of the approaching cavalry assumed that the firing was coming from General Wheeler's cavalry. They formed into a line of battle and advanced. Within minutes, there were blue-coated cavalrymen everywhere. Kelly and Bragg fell back. They would occasionally fire a shot to their rear but with a whole mounted regiment in hot pursuit their primary concern was to get out alive. It was a running battle through the streets of Gordon. Miraculously, neither man was hit.

As they went out the east side of Gordon, Kelly and Bragg split up into the woods. Bragg turned south and Kelly turned north. Bragg got away clean. Kelly, however, not having a leg to help with the turning horse, lost his balance and fell. Within minutes, he was surrounded by Union cavalrymen and taken prisoner.

He was taken back to Gordon. Somewhat oddly, he was told that he would be shot in ten days' time. He was questioned about Wheeler's cavalry and the topography of the area. He was put into an ambulance, without his crutches, and moved with the army as they crossed the Oconee River. For several days, he listened as the band played the Dead March for his benefit. He was taken near Toomsboro and Sandersville. Later, during the night, as they made preparations to cross the Ogeechee River and the nearby swamps, Kelly made his move.

He rolled out of the back of the ambulance and crawled and hopped off into a swamp. He used broken branches for crutches and hobbled, crawled, and dragged himself as far away from his captors as he could. Now, he faced a new danger. He was soaking wet, in a swamp, and it was the end of November in one of the coldest Novembers on record. He was freezing. Death by hypothermia was a very real possibility. Off in the distance he saw the light of a fire. He knew that around the fire might be Yankee soldiers. But he had no real choice. If he stayed in the swamp he would die. He had to risk recapture.

The men at the campfire were completely surprised to find a one-legged man, shivering and covered with mud, come staggering out of the swamp. To his great good fortune, Kelly had come upon some refugees hiding from Sherman's army. Kelly remained with them for several days. When the Yankee army had passed, the refugees left their hiding place and returned to civilization.

Kelly never again went to war. The war had passed him by. He married, raised a family and taught school at the Turner School, three miles northwest of Gordon, for fifty years. He died at Danville, Georgia, on September 19, 1928. He is buried in the cemetery of Liberty Hill Methodist Church in Twiggs County.

# A Yankee Replaces the Organ
## at St. Stephen's Church

W HEN MEMBERS OF THE UNION army were in Milledgeville in November of 1864, they committed many acts of violence toward property. The State House was thoroughly plundered; the State Arsenal was blown up; fences, outbuildings and outhouses were consumed for firewood. The penitentiary was also burned (see photo on page 68). The list of vandalism, theft and simple destruction goes on and on.

One of the more curious incidents of destruction took place in St. Stephen's Episcopal Church. It could be expected that the pews were burned for firewood and the contents and interior were vandalized. The damage done to the building from the explosion which destroyed the nearby arsenal was unavoidable. What seems peculiar is that, in such a cold November, the Yankees had the patience to pour molasses, which would have been very thick and slow-moving, down the organ pipes. But, perhaps they had nothing more interesting at the moment to do, so they spent their time watching the molasses slowly drip into the organ.

After the vandals left the city, the congregation repaired the building, constructed new pews and tidied up. To the best of their ability they cleaned the molasses out of the organ. But they never were able to get it completely repaired and working properly. For the next forty-five years, the church struggled with the sticky organ.

To the surprise of everyone, the solution to the long-standing organ problem was solved by eleven-year-old Nylic Bland. Nylic was the daughter of Marshal and Ruby Bland. Ruby was the church organist. Marshal was the local representative of the New York Life Insurance Company. This man was more than commonly devoted to his employer, so much so that he named his daughter with the initials of the New York Life Insurance Company.

In 1909, young Nylic wrote a letter to George W. Perkins of New York. She explained that in 1864, a New York regiment had damaged the church organ. Using the language of a little girl, she asked Mr. Perkins if he would care to contribute to a fund for purchasing a new organ for the church.

Mr. Perkins, although a former executive officer and member of the Board of Directors of the New York Life Insurance Company, was not at that time connected with the firm. He was, however, a financier with J.P. Morgan & Company and a major power on Wall Street. He was fabulously wealthy. When he died in 1920, his estate was estimated at between $10 and $20 million. He was also a philanthropist.

Little Nylic Bland received a telegram from George W. Perkins. "Buy the organ and send the bill to me." The church bought a new organ for $2,100 and Mr. Perkins, the Yankee, paid the bill.

# Ezekiel Roberts:
# Physician, Highwayman,
# Convict and Captain

Sherlock Holmes said, "When a doctor goes wrong he is the first of criminals. He has nerve and he has knowledge." The comment applies very well to the shadowy figure of Dr. Ezekiel A. Roberts. Little is known of Roberts's early years, although he may have been born about 1816 in Columbia County, Georgia. Where or when he obtained his education and became a physician is unknown.

In the late 1840s he was operating in north Georgia as a highwayman and burglar. He was referred to as a "dangerous criminal" and a "terrible public enemy" in the newspapers. About 1852, he was captured and brought to justice in Monroe County. Roberts was convicted of burglary, roguery and vagabondism. He appealed to the Supreme Court but the court affirmed the decision of the lower court. He was sentenced to twelve years' imprisonment in the penitentiary at Milledgeville. He began his sentence in August of 1853. Inside those bleak walls he remained, year in and year out, until November of 1864.

In late August, a labor force of four or five hundred slaves was working on earthen defenses around Milledgeville. The cadets of Georgia Military Institute were ordered from the trenches of Atlanta to bolster the defenses of Milledgeville. They joined Talbird's Mounted Scouts, Williams's company of militia, the factory and the penitentiary guards and Pruden's battery of artillery. Stores and businesses in Milledgeville were ordered to close at 5:00 p.m. daily. "All residents and refugees" in Milledgeville were required, by order of the governor, to go to the State House grounds for mandatory parades. They would be instructed in the use of artillery pieces and rifles. These citizen soldiers would also be given familiarization tours of the defensive trench system around Milledgeville. Any persons who failed to appear would "be at once sent to the Front." In almost every case, these men were either very young, very old, infirm or otherwise exempt from service in the Georgia militia.

In November, to supply even more manpower to the ranks, Governor Brown looked to the penitentiary. After giving the convicts a patriotic speech, he invited them to form a company to defend Georgia from the advancing army of General Sherman. In return for their military service, the convicts would be given pardons on the condition that they performed satisfactorily. About 150 convicts accepted the offer. They elected forty-eight-year-old Dr. Ezekiel Roberts, the notorious burglar, to be their captain. Dressed in their black-and-white-striped prison uniforms, the convicts paraded with the cadets and local militia groups.

The trenches at Milledgeville were never used. As General Sherman's army approached, it became obvious that the motley five hundred men and boys would not be able to withstand twenty or thirty thousand veteran Yankee troops. They were ordered to Gordon, twenty miles south, on Saturday, November 19, 1864. Milledgeville was being rapidly abandoned by the legislature, the governor and most of the male population.

At Gordon, the various units were under command of Major Francis W. Capers, the superintendent of Georgia Military Institute. Major General Henry C. Wayne, formerly of the U.S. Army and son of a U.S. Supreme Court Justice, was in overall command. On Sunday, November 20, the telegraph line to Macon was cut. Throughout Sunday and Monday, General Wayne received reports and rumors of Yankees approaching from the west. Cut off from his superiors, Wayne determined that he would move his force to the east along the railroad line to the railroad bridge crossing the Oconee River. At 4:00 p.m., with the last of his men boarding the train, he was hastened on his way by bullets from the Federals as they entered Gordon.

Two and a half hours later, the train reached the Oconee River bridge. A guard of 186 men was already there. They were a company of Heyward's South Carolina Cavalry, two pieces of artillery, and a company of the Twenty-seventh Battalion of Georgia Reserves. While at the bridge, Wayne received orders to hold the bridge "to the last extremity."

The bridge could be flanked on either side: on the right from Milledgeville and on the left at Balls Ferry, about three miles downstream. It could also be attacked from the front. All was relatively quiet on Tuesday. On Wednesday, an attack began at the bridge in the morning. About noon, General Wayne received a report that enemy infantry had crossed the river at Balls Ferry. He immediately sent several of his units on a forced march to the south to engage the enemy and drive them back over the river. Captain Roberts's Guards, as they were now called, formed one of the units chosen for that mission.

After some difficult fighting, two to three hundred of the enemy were driven back across the river. Roberts's Guards and Talbots's cavalry were left at Balls Ferry to keep the enemy from crossing again. The enemy assaulted Roberts's Guards and Talbots's cavalry with artillery and rifle fire. An officer wrote later that "the convicts were dressed in prison garb, and were hardened in appearance, but calm and brave." Friday evening, November 25, it was reported to General Wayne that the enemy was preparing to cross the river above and below Balls Ferry and that ammunition was running low. If the men were not withdrawn, they would be killed or captured. Wayne ordered the positions at Balls Ferry abandoned. The convicts of Roberts's Guards as well as the other units rejoined General Wayne and all retreated eastward on the railway.

Major George Ward Nichols, aide-de-camp to Sherman, commented on the convicts, saying that "most of these desperadoes have been taken prisoners, dressed in their state prison clothing. General Sherman has turned them loose, believing that Governor Brown has not got the full benefits of his liberality."

The scenario of skirmishes and withdrawals was repeated time after time as the Federal army pushed the Confederates back into the defenses of Savannah. The Confederate forces withdrew from Savannah before it was given up to General Sherman. Roberts's Guards returned to Milledgeville at the end of December 1864, after spending some time guarding the arsenal and government storehouses at Augusta. They were given a thirty-day furlough. Major General Henry Wayne wrote in his official report that "Roberts Guards generally behaved well. Their captain (Roberts) is a brave and daring man. I recommend them for the full pardon conditionally promised."

About half of the convicts returned from their furlough at the end of January 1865. At this point Dr. Roberts, or Captain Roberts as he would be rightly called, vanished into the mists of history without a trace.

# Transporting Dead Bodies
## During the Civil War

A GRIM FACT OF THE CIVIL War, or any war, is that people die. Many of these people die far from their homes. Often it was the wish of the deceased, or their families, that their bodies be returned to their local community for burial. Obviously, transporting bodies in many cases was impossible, or at the best, impractical and difficult. Besides finding available space on scarce freight cars or wagons during wartime, there were the added difficulties involved with the preservation and packaging of the bodies. This was especially true during warmer weather.

Some bodies were transported, however. In Milledgeville, there are several examples. Andrew J. Micklejohn, Milledgeville's first battle casualty, was killed at Fort Pickens near Pensacola, November 24, 1861. His body was returned to Milledgeville where it was interred with full military honors on November 30.

Robert Memminger Campbell died September 17, 1862, at the battle of Sharpsburg, but his remains were not returned to Milledgeville until November 1866. Captain Jesse Beall was killed at Knoxville, Tennessee on November 30, 1863. His remains were re-interred in Milledgeville in March of 1866. As years had passed since these deaths, and the war had ended, the difficulties involved in these cases would have been different from those where death was more recent. After the war, large numbers of remains were recovered from various battlefields, usually by state governments, and reburied elsewhere.

Georgia Military Institute cadet John McLeod died August 27, 1864, at Milledgeville in the home of General Stith Myrick. Myrick had opened his home to patients of Brown Hospital. Despite this critical period in the war, McLeod's remains were shipped to his home in Burke County for burial. McLeod is the only known instance of remains from Brown Hospital being transported out of town, however. The others were buried in Memory Hill Cemetery.

Newspapers during the war often mentioned the problems, and suggested solutions, for the transportation of bodies. In August of 1862, the *Georgia Journal and Messenger* of Macon, reported that, "A body had been brought here by railroad…from Atlanta, on its way to Dooly county, and had become so offensive that further transportation was refused." The body, in whatever shipping container it was in, was left at the depot and the train continued on. Local authorities took charge of the body and buried it.

The *Richmond Dispatch and Whig* described the situation in detail:

> *We daily observe at the railway stations boxes containing the bodies of deceased soldiers, which have been disinterred by their friends, under the belief that they can be sent off without delay, either by mail train or express. This, however, is an error. Freight trains only carry them, and the detention frequently causes the bodies to become offensive, when their immediate burial by the wayside is a matter of necessity. It would be better to postpone disinterment until cold weather, when it can be accomplished with less trouble and more certainty of getting the remains of the departed to their destination. Metallic coffins are difficult to obtain, and wooden ones can only be procured by the payment of a large sum. In these the dead bodies are packed with sawdust, and in warm weather their transportation to a distant point is uncertain, if not absolutely impossible.*

The *Georgia Journal and Messenger* reprinted the article from the *Richmond Dispatch and Whig* and offered a solution to the problem:

> *To the above we have to add, (and that from personal knowledge) that nothing is more easy, convenient, or cheap than transporting bodies at any season of the year, to any distance. Any common coffin will answer. Have a piece of cotton osnaburg or other cloth of the necessary size — dip it in boiling tar, and wrap the coffin in it and it is sealed tighter than it can be done in a metallic case. Place it in a box with some kind of packing to keep it from moving, and the work is complete. No charcoal, or disinfectant is necessary.*

The *Georgia Journal and Messenger* article was widely reprinted. There is no way of knowing if the described method was often utilized. This topic, however objectionable, clearly was of interest to a great many people.

# SON, THAT LEG HAS TO COME OFF...

S EVERAL MEN WHO SERVED IN the Confederate army from Milledgeville received wounds that required amputation. It is a very sobering fact that, in the Union army, thirty thousand amputations were performed. There are no statistics for the Confederate army, but doubtless a similar number of amputations were performed by Confederate surgeons.

Because of the large number of amputations performed, surgeons early in the war got the reputation for being eager to amputate. This may have been due to their operating outdoors, where the surgeries were more likely to be seen. Also, laymen did not realize that if they were struck in a party of the body other than the head or torso, a bullet or artillery shell fragment would cause shocking damage to bones and tissue. Amputation simply was the only way to treat such severe injuries to limbs. In fact, studies made during and after the war concluded that far more lives could have been saved if amputations had been carried out rather than attempts made to save injured limbs.

When we think of amputations or surgery in the Civil War, we may visualize a scene in which a patient is being operated on without the benefit of anesthetics, biting on a bullet and being held down and screaming. Though popular with Hollywood, this was not the case. Anesthetics were almost always used. However, one of the side effects of ether or chloroform was that the patient would be unconscious yet in a state of excitement, causing him to shout and writhe on the operating table. With outdoor operations, visible to many, such a scene would lead the observer to believe that the patient was conscious and in extreme pain. Reports of such operations were frequently sent home in letters and appeared in the newspapers.

The military medical departments of both sides were woefully unprepared for the tremendous number of battle casualties. In the first year of the war, it was frequent for the wounded not to receive any care for a day or more. This delay greatly increased the risk of infection and death. In the case of amputations, the sooner the operation was performed, the more likely the patient would survive. The percentage of deaths occurring after treatment dropped tremendously with improved evacuation, transportation and hospital organization. After Sharpsburg, 22 percent of the 8,112 wounded Union soldiers died. After Gettysburg, one year later, only 9 percent of 10,569 died. Figures are unavailable for Confederate wounded, but similar reductions are likely.

My own great-great-grandfather, Captain Alfred Flournoy Zachry, Company F, Sixty-first Alabama Infantry, had his left arm amputated after being wounded on May 12, 1864, at Spotsylvania. His amputation took place the following day.

James E. Hanger, an eighteen-year-old private, of Company D, Twenty-third Virginia Infantry, was the first soldier to undergo an amputation in the Civil War. He was at the battle of Philippi, June 3, 1861, when he was struck by an artillery shell. He was captured and a Union surgeon amputated his leg. He was exchanged a couple of months later. His career as a soldier was over. While he was recuperating, he experimented with various means of constructing an artificial leg with the principal use of barrel staves and rubber.

His artificial leg was successful. He started to make what he called "The Hanger Limb" for other soldiers who had lost legs. He was granted Patent Number 155 by the Confederate Patent Office, March 23, 1863, for his artificial leg. He kept on experimenting, and on August 18, 1863, he was granted another patent for an improved artificial leg. The state of Virginia commissioned Hanger to design and build "Hanger Legs" for Confederate soldiers. He opened a clinic in Richmond.

In 1862, the U.S. government guaranteed prostheses for veterans who lost arms or legs during the war. Throughout the war, entrepreneurs and inventors of all persuasions, from charlatans to honest inventors, tried to make better artificial limbs. With such huge casualty lists, it was an enormous market and many wanted to become involved in the business.

In 1866, a bill was passed in Georgia to provide prosthetic arms and legs to indigent soldiers. Other Southern states provided similar relief to their veterans. While the U.S. government provided devices to all amputees, this benefit did not apply to soldiers of the Confederacy. Each Southern state had to provide for its own veterans.

Unfortunately, there is no evidence regarding any of the Milledgeville amputees receiving prosthetic devices.

For the next fifty years, state governments supplied artificial limbs to veterans of the Civil War. It was big business. James E. Hanger's firm prospered. In fact, it is still in existence as Hanger Orthopedic Group, Inc., and is one of the largest manufacturers of prosthetic limbs in the world.

# THE CONFEDERATE MONUMENT ON
# MILLEDGEVILLE'S JEFFERSON STREET

IN 1910, THE CIVIL WAR had been over for forty-five years. The number of living veterans was decreasing and two generations had grown up in the postwar period. The memories of the war, the reasons it was fought and the recognition for the participants was fading.

The situation was very similar to that faced by the organizers of the World War II Memorial in Washington, D.C., ninety years later. A monument was needed to commemorate the spirit, sacrifice and commitment the people of Georgia displayed during the Civil War. There had been a simple obelisk monument in Memory Hill Cemetery since 1868; now a more elaborate monument was wanted.

The local R.E. Lee Chapter of the United Daughters of the Confederacy took up the challenge and began to raise funds for a monument to the private soldiers of the Confederacy. Their goal was to "perpetuate the memory of the daring bravery of the Confederate soldiers." The *Union-Recorder* wholeheartedly endorsed the project and urged "every man, woman and child in this city and county" to "contribute something to the success of this movement."

Joseph E. Pottle, a veteran of the Spanish-American War and Commander of the D.B. Sanford, Sons of Confederate Veterans Camp, wrote an eloquent appeal which was printed in the February 22, 1910 *Union-Recorder*. He stated that "a land without memories is a land without history, without a future, without hope...the old Confederate States of America have the greatest motive to be proud of the unselfish devotion, the unrivalled courage of their sons and of their daughters." It was they who *fought and suffered and sacrificed for the highest and holiest ideal…Here, in this city, the central city of the storm-swept section, in the heart of the territory which Sherman and his cohorts left in ashes and despair, is seen no memorial of our fathers valor…surely it is impossible that the good women of this county, whose fathers, whose husbands, whose loved ones lie dead upon the field of battle, will call in vain upon the children of the dead to help them send up, to be kissed by Southern breezes, a shaft of marble to the memory of the dead.*

Pottle continued,

*these women are full of zeal, of courage and of patriotism. To the women of the South must our posterity look to keep the fires of patriotism burning on our altars. I assert that every man, however poor, every woman, however humble, every child, however obscure, whose veins bear the blood of our devoted dead, who lives in this county, should esteem it a privilege and an honor to assist in the work of building this monument. Every father should teach his son to stand before it with bowed head, every mother should bring her daughter to look up to this outward testimony of faith in our fathers and our mothers sacrificial offering, to our Country's honor.* [When the veterans are all dead]*the monument will rise to testify to the world that the hearts of their sons and daughters to the remotest generations will quicken with reverence and with love to the memory of the greatest soldiers who ever donned a uniform, to the most self sacrificing and courageous people who ever battled against ever increasing odds for home, for honor and for truth. Let us all come, therefore, with our plenty and with our pittance and pay this last homage to the memory of the martyred dead.*

The money came in but slowly. It was over a year later, in April 1911, that it was announced that the monument had been ordered. It was to be unveiled on Robert E. Lee's birthday, January 19, 1912. The announcement included another plea for more donations to the monument fund.

January 1912 came and went. It is unknown whether the monument simply was not finished in time for Lee's birthday or if the ladies had not raised enough money to pay for it. In late February, a notice appeared in the newspaper saying that the monument would be located in the center of the intersection of Hancock and Wilkinson Streets and unveiled on Memorial Day, April 26. Thousands of people were expected to attend the unveiling.

On Friday, April 26, 1912, at 11:00 a.m., the elderly Civil War veterans were escorted by the Baldwin Blues and the cadet battalion from Georgia Military College to Memory Hill Cemetery. Flowers were laid upon the graves of the "sleeping heroes" and salutes were fired.

The veterans returned to the courthouse where they were the honored guests at a luncheon served by the members of the R.E. Lee Chapter of the United Daughters of the Confederacy.

At 2:30 p.m., the unveiling of the new monument took place. All stores were closed and a huge crowd formed in the streets to witness the historic event. Colonel John A. Sibley was master of ceremonies. The first item on the program was a song sung by the students of Georgia Normal and Industrial College, now Georgia College & State University. Regrettably, the name of the song is not known.

A prayer followed the singing. After prayer, "The Boys in Gray are Growing Old" was sung by the male quartet of C.I. Brown, Charles Conn, Bardy Tant (the elder half-brother of Oliver Hardy of "Laurel and Hardy" fame) and Erwin Sibley. This was followed by an address by Colonel Joseph E. Pottle. Pottle spoke without notes and as he talked he became more and more intense. It was said that "his eloquence held his hearers well nigh spell bound." The address was followed by a "bugle call," which likely was "Taps."

The monument was then unveiled by the following young ladies: Josie Sibley, Mary Pottle, Isabel Allen, Maggie Bivins, Jessie Allen, Josephine Bethune, Frances Roberts, Margaret Joseph, Mary Horne, Sarah Frances Edwards and Caro Lane.

To the delight of the crowd, the girls of GN & IC then sang "Dixie" with the crowd joining in on the chorus. A collection was then taken up as the monument still was not fully funded.

Crosses of Honor were presented to the veterans J.A. Buck, J.E. Gholson, Tomlinson Fort Newell, Mark H. McComb, L.J. Smith and George T. Whilden. "Hooray for the Sunny South" was then sung by the quartet and the students of GMC.

Camp Doles, No. 730, United Confederate Veterans, publicly thanked the ladies for their accomplishment of bringing the Confederate Monument into existence. They said, "it will stand as monument to *their* memory as well as to the heroism of the Confederate dead. The sentinels thereon will keep their silent watch until the last bugle shall sound."

In 1949, the Confederate Monument was removed from the intersection of Hancock and Wilkinson Streets and placed on Jefferson Street across from the north gate of Georgia Military College.

# GEORGIA MILITARY
# INSTITUTE CADETS

F OUNDED IN 1852 AT MARIETTA, Georgia, the Georgia Military Institute (GMI) was
only marginally popular as a military or educational institution until the late 1850s
when the specter of the Civil War loomed on the horizon. In the late spring of 1861,
the student enrollment became quite low as many cadets enlisted in the ranks of the
Confederate army. Those cadets who did not enlist were utilized as drill instructors at
many training camps across the state.

As the war continued, the Confederacy began to draft men into the army. To the
dismay of eager young cadets, Governor Joseph E. Brown (see photo on page 66)
was determined to keep the faculty and cadets of GMI exempt from Confederate
conscription. Governor Brown and Confederate President Jefferson Davis were at odds
regarding the status of cadets. Brown finally secured the cadets permanent exemption
by appointing GMI Superintendent Major Francis W. Capers to the position of Chief
Engineer of the State of Georgia. Brown then declared the GMI cadets to be "the
Engineer Corps of the State."

Protected from conscription, the school was flooded with applications for admission
from wealthy parents seeking a haven where their sons would not be called into Confederate
service. The school acquired somewhat of a reputation among civilians and soldiers as a
refuge for draft dodgers. Governor Brown's Georgia state militia became known as "Joe
Brown's Pets" for much the same reason. The motivation of my great-grandfather, William
Henry Harrington, is unknown, but he was a corporal in Company A of the GMI cadets.

The cadets themselves were eager to get into battle. They would write letters to
newspapers and to Governor Brown suggesting that they could do more service in
the active military than at their studies. Some suggested that Governor Brown was

keeping the cadets out of action, as his sixteen-year-old son, Julius, was a member of the cadet corps.

At the end of May 1864, with Sherman's army bearing down on Atlanta, the cadets were ordered to take the train to West Point, Georgia. Their mission was to guard the railroad bridge over the Chattahoochee River. They remained there for a month.

At the end of July, the cadets were ordered to the trenches around Atlanta. The trenches they manned were near the location of present-day Houston and Boulevard streets. There, they participated in the hazardous duty of the battle of Atlanta and lost several cadets to disease as well as enemy fire. Cadet Samuel W. Goode was the first battle casualty when he was struck in the shoulder by a bullet on August 7. The next afternoon two cadets were at a campfire cooking bacon when a cannonball landed nearby and then passed through the body of cadet Archibald H. Alexander of Monroe County, killing him almost instantly. That day, August 8, was my great-grandfather's eighteenth birthday, no doubt a birthday he would always remember. Three cadets—W. Baker, J. Mabry and G. Smith—became sick and died of typhoid within a few days. Thirty percent of the cadets would get sick, wounded or die in the defense of Atlanta.

On August 12, 1864, the cadets were ordered to Milledgeville to participate in the defense of the capital. Arriving on the sixteenth, they found their first quarters to be empty boxcars at the Milledgeville depot. After that they encamped in tents on the northeast corner of State House square. Major Capers was appointed commandant of all the troops at Milledgeville. His command included the cadets, Captain Pruden's artillery battery, and Captain Talbot's company of Georgia State Line cavalry.

Milledgeville was home for several of the cadets, including Julius Brown, the son of the governor, as well as Lyman H. Compton, Lucius James Lamar, Goodwin Dowdell Myrick and James Dowdell Myrick.

On August 27, 1864, the cadets lost two of their comrades to typhoid contracted in the trenches of Atlanta. Cadet John McLeod died at the home of General Stith Myrick and Cadet Ringold Commander died at the home of Robert A. McComb.

In Milledgeville, the cadets drilled, guarded the state armory and attended classes. The schoolwork soon fell by the wayside as military activity came closer. On September 2, Atlanta fell to General Sherman. With Atlanta secured, Sherman looked south and east for his next conquests. By the middle of November, it was apparent that Milledgeville was a target. Adjutant General Henry Wayne assumed command in Milledgeville, adding to the existing troops companies from the factory and penitentiary guards, a local militia company made up of old, infirm and very young men, plus a company of paroled convicts from the penitentiary. Hundreds of slaves built earthworks around Milledgeville. However, when it was determined that thirty thousand veteran Union troops were approaching Milledgeville, it was clear that the five hundred ragtag defenders could not resist them. The school days for the GMI cadets were over for good.

On Saturday, November 19, the cadets and the other defenders of Milledgeville entrained for Gordon twenty miles south. While Milledgeville was targeted by the left wing of Sherman's army, the right wing made a feint toward Macon and then turned to the east to cross the Oconee River south of Milledgeville. The right wing would go through the little town of Gordon. Faced with another army of thirty thousand enemy soldiers, General Wayne fell back from Gordon along the railroad tracks to the Oconee River Bridge on Monday November 21. Here he would make a stand.

On Tuesday, the cadets dug in on the west side of the Oconee River. Other units, from General Wayne's irregular forces, were sent to the north and south along the river to prevent the Union army from crossing. Uniting with forces already at the bridge, including elements of the Fourth Kentucky, Wayne's little band now amounted to 646 men, including convicts, local militia, cavalry, artillery and cadets. That night the temperature dropped to twelve degrees and brought snow, which made the night on the defensive line miserable.

On Wednesday morning, the Union attack on the bridge began. The cadets performed well. Captain Weller of the Fourth Kentucky said, "the cadets were, of course very young, some of them certainly not over fourteen years of age. The Federals advanced their line of skirmishers, and firing commenced. The bravery of the school boys was the glory of this fight. Several of their number were carried off wounded and dying. I can never forget the looks of one little boy as four convicts carried him on a stretcher to the rear. His handsome young face, with the flush of fever on it, and the resolute expression of his eyes, indicated that he fully realized the situation." Cadet Clayton H. Marsh was mortally wounded. Cadet Scott Todd was shot in the arm, which was later amputated at the shoulder. There were other casualties as well. Facing overwhelming opposition, they were forced to slowly retreat back across the bridge. They dug in again on the east side of the river. The cadets faced several determined attacks and sporadic rifle fire as well as artillery fire all day. Thursday, November 24, another cold day, brought more Federal attacks on the bridge as well as the river crossings above and below the bridge. Toward evening the west end of the bridge was set on fire by the enemy.

The fire burned all day Friday while the enemy fire kept the cadets from re-crossing the bridge to put it out. During the afternoon, it became apparent that the enemy was no longer opposing them. The fire was then extinguished. Reports started coming in that huge numbers of the enemy had crossed the river to the north and more were preparing to cross to the south. The bridge had to be abandoned or the defenders would be cut off and captured. The cadets and the other units pulled back along the railway line at 1:00 a.m. on Saturday, November 26, after having held off the Union army for a few precious days.

By December 6, the little band of militiamen, school boys and convicts who had started out to defend Milledgeville were pressed into the defenses of Savannah. Along the way they had many small skirmishes with the unstoppable Union army.

When Savannah was evacuated the cadets marched to Bamberg, South Carolina and then took a train to Augusta, arriving on December 26 "almost naked and half starved." In Augusta, the cadets, convicts and militia were fed on half rations of "poor beef & musty flour." Morale dropped. Many cadets considered resigning from the cadet corps, which would leave them vulnerable to the draft. Desertions from the convict and state militia were common. To make matters worse, it was believed by at least one cadet that Major Capers "stayed drunk in Augusta."

In early February 1865, the cadets returned to Milledgeville. There they again drilled. Apparently they were still eager to fight despite the difficulties of the past months. In April, the cadets hanged Governor Brown in effigy on the State House grounds. They continued to believe that Governor Brown kept them out of the fighting to protect his son, Julius. A witness suggested that the "truth is they ought all to be home in their trundle beds as they are nothing but children."

Children or not, in the last week of April, 1865, the cadets returned to Augusta to guard the arsenal and government storehouses. On May 1, they were called to the Augusta City Hall to quell a riot by paroled Confederate soldiers who were looting government storehouses. With the war at an end, Federal troops entered Augusta on May 3. Two days later the cadets disbanded and each headed for his own home. For my great-grandfather, home was West Point, Georgia. GMI never reopened.

The cadets were the last organized Confederate soldiers east of the Mississippi.

# WARREN A. MOSELEY, A CONFEDERATE SOLDIER FOR OVER FIFTY YEARS

WARREN ALONZO MOSELEY WAS BORN in Atlanta in 1828. When war came, he was living in Milledgeville in an area known as Moseleyville near the asylum where he worked. In April of 1861, he enlisted as a private in the Baldwin Blues and was soon in Virginia where that unit became Company H, Fourth Georgia Infantry.

In June 1862, he was wounded and captured at Strasburg, Virginia. He was exchanged at Point Lookout, Maryland, in September 1862. In April 1863, he was transferred to Company A, Fourth Georgia Reserve Cavalry, where he was elected captain. In May 1863, he was wounded at Chancellorsville, Virginia.

After that time, he returned to Georgia. His primary duties were in north Georgia, where his cavalry unit fought against roaming bands of deserters, outlaws and bushwhackers from both armies. In the spring of 1865, he surrendered at Milledgeville.

However, for Warren Moseley, the war wasn't over. Not that he kept fighting the war. He had surrendered and his days of combat were over. However, he never would forget his service to the Confederacy. The memory of that service, the scenes he had witnessed, and the camaraderie he had enjoyed became the highlights of the rest of his life. In a way, he became like some of today's college football fans. Their time at the college may be many years in the past, but the fans still loyally follow the team, reminisce about teams of long ago and keenly exchange news and information about their favorite sport.

After the war, Moseley found employment on the police force of Macon. He worked there very successfully for the rest of his long life. He married and raised a family. However, the war and his part in it played a major role in his future.

Whenever there was a reunion or another event in which veterans talked about battles, campaigns, generals or strategy, Captain Moseley was either there or wanted to be there. At one reunion a newspaper said that Captain Moseley would be there and would "wear the coat which shows by its numerous bullet holes the number of wounds he received during the war."

Moseley could tell a story as well as anyone. A few of his stories follow.

In 1900, a newspaper carried a story he told of the "hoodoo hat." Moseley is referred to as "one of the bravest of the boys who went out in the sixties." According to the story, at the battle of Winchester, Virginia, a Yankee soldier was killed very near the line of battle and a Confederate soldier picked up the dead man's hat and wore it. A couple of hours later the man was shot in the head; the bullet went through the same hole in the hat that the bullet that killed the Yankee had gone through. Another soldier picked up the hat and wore it. An hour later, he too was killed by a bullet going through the same hole in the hat. The following day, yet another soldier was wearing the hat when he was struck by a bullet passing through the same hole in the hat. The story concludes by saying that though this hat "was a fine one," no one would wear it any longer.

In 1904, an advertisement appeared in several Northern newspapers. It was an ad for Duffy's Pure Malt Whiskey. The headline of the ad stated that "Famous Confederate Veterans Use and Recommend" Duffy's product. Captain Moseley is referred to as the "hero of the Bloody Angle and Cedar Creek." Moseley is quoted as saying,

> I never felt better in my life, and I owe it all to Duffy's Pure Malt Whiskey. I was wounded eight times during the war and after General Lee's surrender returned home completely broken down. My wounds gave me a good deal of trouble, and I had attacks of extreme weakness, with great loss of blood. Doctors said nothing would enrich my blood and build me up so quickly and thoroughly as Duffy's Pure Malt Whiskey. I took nothing else. Although past 65, I am in perfect physical and mental condition and devote twelve hours a day to my business.

He may have been laughing pretty hard when he gave that endorsement. Or, maybe after sufficient quantities of the whiskey, he was feeling especially good. We will never know.

A letter appeared in the *Atlanta Constitution* from a man seeking the words to the poem "Lee to the Rear." This poem is about an incident at the Battle of the Wilderness. General Lee was about to lead an attack on a Union position when he was stopped by a private. The private said that he and the others would make the assault but that Lee must remain in the rear. Warren Moseley's wife wrote to the newspaper, supplied a copy of the entire poem and commented that her husband "remembers the incident."

The 1905 veterans' reunion in Macon was a special opportunity for Moseley. Several days before the event, the newspapers reported that Moseley had "devoted months to preparation" and "the fact that Captain Moseley will be in charge [of the parade] is assurance of a most interesting affair."

According to the *Atlanta Constitution*, three thousand veterans showed up for the two-day event. Twenty thousand spectators lined the street, "waving their hats, canes, umbrellas and handkerchiefs." The newspaper went on to state that

> *When the parade was over, Captain Moseley formed his cavalry at the foot of Cherry Street, in Macon. The mounted men charged up to Cotton Avenue. All the old men in this troop rode, as in their younger days, and they seemed to warm up to that ragged heat of excitement always evident among the men on the eve of battle. The war whoop sounded and the men were off. At breakneck speed, they dashed down the paved street, flashing old-time sabers. The crowds fell in behind them and yelled themselves hoarse.*

It must have been quite a scene and Warren Moseley was there in the thick of it, enjoying every moment.

Besides personally engaging in reunions, Moseley also was a collector of artifacts. He brought back more than forty pounds of relics gathered from battlefields around Richmond after a trip to a reunion in Virginia. Among other things, he had two minie balls that had struck each other in flight and became lodged in one another. It was said that he had "one of the most complete museums in the state in which he had placed hundreds of relics of the civil war."

Moseley fell on hard times. In 1910, he applied for, and received, a pension from the state of Georgia given to destitute veterans. In his application, he stated that he had no assets and received seventy dollars per month for his work with the city of Macon.

Time finally caught up with the old soldier. He died of the grippe on December 17, 1912. He was buried in Rose Hill Cemetery in Macon. No doubt his old comrades, veterans of the war, stood by the graveside at his funeral. His grave is marked with a simple tombstone. Ironically, however, the tombstone does not indicate that it marks the burial place of a Confederate soldier.

# DAVID R. SNELLING:
# A CASE OF DEFECTION

IT IS PART OF THE natural course of events for an army, any army, to have desertions. Men leave their units for a multitude of reasons. The soldiers of the Confederacy were no exception. Several men from the Baldwin County area deserted. One—Green M. Smith of the Myrick Volunteers, Company G, Forty-fifth Georgia—left the army at Appomattox only hours before the surrender.

While desertion was relatively common, defection was not. Deserters usually just headed for home. Defectors, however, enlisted in the Union army to fight against their former comrades.

The only known defector from the central Georgia area is David R. Snelling. Snelling's parents, Elizabeth Lester and William B. Snelling, lived in the Milledgeville area shortly after 1830. They soon moved to Macon and then to Crawford County. In the early 1840s, William Snelling died. His widow moved with her children to the Fortville area of Jones County. She moved into a house near the large plantations belonging to her brothers, David and Dennis Lester. David Snelling was five years old at that time.

In 1854, Elizabeth Snelling died. She left two surviving children. One was sent to live with an aunt in New Orleans. The other, David Snelling, who was then sixteen, lived and worked for his uncle, David Lester. Apparently, David Snelling was unhappy living with his uncle. One of his cousins was sent to college while he, David, worked in the fields. He never forgot this, which he must have considered an unfair deal.

After a year with his uncle, Snelling moved to the home of Colonel John Singleton, a neighbor. Singleton encouraged Snelling's interest in literature and education. He also arranged for Snelling to live and work for a schoolmaster in Baldwin County. Snelling would work at odd jobs in exchange for his board and tuition. He apparently was adept at scholarship. At the age of twenty-one Snelling went back to Fortville, taking a position as an overseer.

It may be that at this time he developed an aversion to slavery. As an overseer he was exempt from the draft. However, perhaps as part of a larger plan to defect in the future, Snelling enlisted as a private in a company that was being formed in the area by a neighbor, Captain Richard Bonner, in May of 1862. This unit would become Company H, Fifty-seventh Georgia Volunteer Infantry.

In July, while on picket duty near Bridgeport, Alabama, Snelling took a small boat and crossed the Tennessee River into Union-occupied territory. On August 5, he enlisted in the Union Army. He was soon promoted to the rank of lieutenant in Company I, First Alabama Regiment of Union Cavalry.

This regiment was truly diverse. Its ranks were made up of both whites and blacks from nine Southern states, eight Northern states, the border states and eight foreign countries.

David Snelling fought in several engagements while part of his cavalry unit. He was captured once and exchanged. After the fall of Atlanta, during the March to the Sea, Company I with Lieutenant Snelling in command was selected to be General William Tecumseh Sherman's cavalry escort.

On the evening of November 22, 1864, General Sherman was camped along the roadside about ten miles from Milledgeville. For miles around, the night was filled with light from the thousands of campfires of the Union army. An elderly black man came to Sherman and stared at him, wanting to assure himself that the Yankees had come at last. David Snelling, upon seeing this man, recognized him as being a slave on his uncle's plantation, which was about six miles away. The slave was delighted to find his young master returning safe and in a Yankee uniform.

Snelling asked General Sherman for permission to visit his uncle. Permission was granted and Snelling, along with some men, went to the plantation of David Lester. Snelling was not warmly received by his uncle. While his men ransacked the house, Snelling inquired about his friends and relations. He then exchanged his worn-out horse for a better horse belonging to his uncle. As they left with their loot, Snelling's men set fire to David Lester's gin house.

Snelling was honorably discharged on July 19, 1865, at Nashville, Tennessee. He then returned to Georgia and to Milledgeville. He visited with his old friend Colonel Singleton and also his former commander Captain Bonner, who apparently had never bitterly condemned him for his defection. However, the townspeople of Milledgeville were another matter.

In testimony before a Joint Committee on Reconstruction, General George Spencer, who had raised the First Alabama Regiment of Union Cavalry, stated that "[Snelling] returned to Milledgeville, but was allowed to remain only six hours there. He was mobbed in the streets of Milledgeville, and was charged with being responsible for everything that Sherman's whole army did in Milledgeville. His friends and relations made him leave to save his life."

Snelling never returned to Georgia and never corresponded with his Georgia friends or relations. He first went to Huntsville, Alabama, then to Decatur and later to Aberdeen, Mississippi. From there he went to Ozark, Arkansas, where he married a woman named Margaret Nelson in 1880.

He drifted from job to job. He was a school teacher and later a laborer in a cotton gin where he severely injured an arm in the machinery. In 1882, he established a weekly newspaper, the *Ozark Echo*, which failed after a year. He ran for a county office but was not elected. He invented a washing machine but it was not well received and he did not bother to patent it.

He built a six-room house and farmed on a small holding. He also worked as a house painter and paper hanger. He became an alcoholic, but through the insistence and perseverance of his wife he overcame it. He was well respected by the community and often wrote articles for a local newspaper.

He died of bronchial pneumonia April 23, 1901. In 1908, his widow obtained a pension for his service in the Union army. She died in 1944.

Many years after his death, his daughter remembered that he would go on long quiet walks. She described him has being "a tall, thin man, with troubled brown eyes." Snelling left no record of his thoughts on his defection, his return to Milledgeville or his isolation from his friends and relations.

# MILLEDGEVILLE
# THROUGH YANKEE EYES

IN NOVEMBER OF 1864, THIRTY thousand Union soldiers poured through Milledgeville. In three days they were gone. Behind them they left a trail of vandalism, violence, destruction and hatred that may never be entirely erased.

Each of those soldiers witnessed Milledgeville during its hour of crisis. While they all had impressions of the little city of two to three thousand people, only a few notes from those who put their thoughts on paper have survived.

In the words of a Minnesota soldier, Milledgeville was "an ancient, aristocratic place with handsomely shaded trees and dwellings, but it wore an air of quiet decadence and lack of enterprise." To a Wisconsin man, it was "sort of a one-horse town." Another echoed, "We passed through the capital of the state, it is a miserable one-horse city not worthy [of] the name of city."

Major James A. Connolly saw a different Milledgeville. He was impressed with the neat streets and sidewalks covered with sand. He wrote, "The dwellings are scattered and surrounded by large and tastefully decorated grounds." He enjoyed the smell of boxwoods in private gardens. He saw in the attractive and spacious houses a sense of culture and refinement. He was quartered at the home of Dr. William A. Jarratt, located at 131 North Columbia Street, one of the most elegant homes in Milledgeville. From the east bank of the Oconee River, he found himself looking at the poorer areas that gave a "shabby and rickety appearance."

Connolly observed "neatly painted little signboards attached to the buildings or fences" identifying the streets. He also noted mileposts on the road to Sandersville "with notches to mark the miles and half notches to indicate half miles."

The State House, in Connolly's view, had "rather a superabundance of fancy cornice outside." Finding churches on the State House square surprised him. When he first saw them with their Greek Revival architecture, he thought they were public office buildings.

Sergeant Stephen Fleharty said that while the streets were crowded with blacks in a very festive mood, whites were seldom seen on the streets. He commented that many houses appeared to be closed and vacated. Doubtless many were, and many people remained indoors and kept as low a profile as possible. Referring to Milledgeville he said, "The town is pretty, but aside from the capital building and a few other structures, it is rather insignificant. We have seen no state capital yet that is as small as the capital of Georgia."

An unnamed reporter for the *New York Herald* accompanied Sherman's army. He wrote,

> *The rebel capital is a very pretty little city, capable of accommodating about five thousand inhabitants. It is situated on the Oconee River upon commanding ground, in the heart of a rich and productive agricultural district, in Baldwin county. The residences are nearly all splendid structures, the surroundings of which show the owners to have been people of a high degree of taste and refinement. The gardens of the more wealthy are beautifully laid out; the lawns spacious and beautiful, and the streets clean and well proportioned. In the centre of the town is the Capitol building, a large brown stone building, of modern style of architecture, situated in the centre of a ten acre square, upon the corners of which, and inside of the fence which surrounds the whole, are small, but neatly furnished churches. Outside, and adjacent to the Capitol grounds, are the arsenal and magazine, both very good buildings for the purposes for which they are used. These, the Governors Mansion, and the Milledgeville Hotel, are the chief public buildings of the city.*

Illinois native William F. Saylor, leader of the First Brigade band of the third Division of the Twentieth Corps, wrote his minister father that Milledgeville "contains some beautiful buildings." However, "A great many of the inhabitants had left when we got there [Milledgeville] and the town looked desolate enough. We burned the State Prison [see photo on page 68] and the arsenal and other public buildings and pillaged and plundered the town generally. It was an awful looking place when we got through." Regrettably, this is a view that was likely shared by many.

# INDEX

## Z

www.ingramcontent.com/pod-product-compliance
Lightning Source LLC
Chambersburg PA
CBHW070348100426
42812CB00005B/1458